more petals with less labour

the naturalized garden

D1537674

stephen westcott-gratton

photographs by andrew leyerle

Prentice
Hall
Canada

A Pearson Company

TORONTO

Canadian Cataloguing in Publication Data

Westcott-Gratton, Stephen
    The naturalized garden : More petals with less labour

Includes index.
ISBN 0-13-030571-5

1. Natural landscaping – Canada. 2. Natural landscaping – United States. 3. Low maintenance gardening – Canada. 4. Low maintenance gardening – United States. 5. Gardening to attract wildlife – Canada. 6. Gardening to attract wildlife – United States. 7. Natural gardens – Canada – Design. 8. Natural gardens – United States – Design. I. Leyerle, Andrew. II. Title.

SB439.26.C3W47 2001   635.9'0971   C00-932919-6

ISBN 0-13-030571-5

Editorial Director, Trade Division: Andrea Crozier
Acquisitions Editor: Andrea Crozier
Managing Editor: Tracy Bordian
Copy Editor: Wendy Thomas
Art Direction: Mary Opper
Cover and Interior Design: Mary Opper
Cover Photo: © 2001 Andrew Leyerle
Production Manager: Kathrine Pummell
Page Layout: Kyle Gell Design

1 2 3 4 5 Transcontinental 05 04 03 02 01

Printed and bound in Canada.

ATTENTION: CORPORATIONS
Books are available at quantity discounts with bulk purchase for educational, business, or sales promotional use. For information, please email or write to: Pearson PTR Canada, Special Sales, PTR Division, 26 Prince Andrew Place, Don Mills, Ontario, M3C 2T8. Email: ss.corp@pearsoned.com. Please supply: title of book, ISBN, quantity, how the book will be used, date needed.

Visit the Pearson PTR Canada Web site! Send us your comments, browse our catalogues, and more.
www.pearsonptr.ca

Prentice
Hall
Canada
A Pearson Company

in memory of
Daniel Hall Pearse
(1947–1991)
my horticultural mentor

contents

PREFACE VII

[1] getting grounded 1

LEARNING FROM THE PAST, PLANNING FOR
THE FUTURE

[2] getting started, keeping going 15

WHAT EVERY NATURAL GARDENER
NEEDS TO KNOW

[3] the woodland garden 37

A FOREST OF PETALS

[4] the meadow garden 77

INTRODUCING COLOUR TO THE
GRASSLANDS

[5] the damp garden 111

SUNDRY BLOOMS FOR THE BOG

APPENDIX: PLANT & CATALOGUE SOURCE LIST 136

GLOSSARY 141

HARDINESS ZONES 144

GARDEN CREDITS 145

INDEX 146

preface

the natural garden:
a definition for the 21st century

The most important aim of a naturalized garden is to create a balanced mini-ecosystem right on the *terra firma* you call home. Natural gardens should be beautiful to behold, ecologically friendly, and low maintenance. Understanding the premise of nature's scheme by choosing suitable plant material for your garden's own conditions will ensure that you succeed without having to resort to an arsenal of synthetic chemical additives. Naturalized gardening is more a method or technique of gardening rather than a specific garden style. Re-creating a woodland garden, planting a prairie meadow, or arranging drifts of flowers to attract birds, butterflies, and beneficial insects to your garden — the possibilities are endless!

getting
grounded

*Naturalizing spring bulbs in turfgrass is a good way
to get the best of both worlds. Star-of-Bethlehem
(Ornithogalum nutans, pictured here), a Eurasian
native and hardy from Zones 5 to 9, is one of the more
vigorous species, but snowdrops (Galanthus nivalis),
Siberian squill (Scilla siberica), and striped squill
(Puschkinia scilloides) are also excellent choices.*

Over the years, the term "naturalized" has been used to describe a number of different gardening styles. Several hundred years ago it would have meant an open parkland replete with constructed lakes and strategically placed trees, while in recent years it might have signified a strictly native plant garden. Neither of these extremes provides appropriate solutions for busy twenty-first century gardeners who crave a sea of petals every bit as much as their neighbours do, but who have a limited amount of time to spend maintaining their real estate. This book will show you how to get the maximum bloom out of your garden with the minimum input of time and energy.

Like most people who have been gardening on the same plot of land for a number of years, a few years ago I began to notice that some plants were taking over certain areas of the garden while others dwindled and eventually disappeared. It was this phenomenon, so characteristic of plant groups in the wild, that first attracted me to the "natural gardening" style.

When I started to garden in earnest, I wanted to try to grow every plant I possibly could that was hardy in my zone, so before long, I ended up with what could be politely described as a collector's garden, but what was, in reality, a bit of a hodgepodge. I already knew about individual plant preferences for sun or shade and moist or dry soil, so I was off to a good start, but it soon became apparent that plants (like people) vary enormously in their vigour and stamina. As I became busier with my career and had less and less time to spend in my own garden, it was these no-fuss, robust plants that I became increasingly enamoured with at the expense of the garden invalids who often required chemical tonics to keep them going.

Of course, there's a difference between a robust plant and an invasive one. Invasive plants are a no-no and are largely responsible for giving plants from other countries a bad name. In North American terms, a "native" plant is one that was growing here before Europeans arrived, and any plant that has been introduced since is technically an "exotic" or "alien." But here's the rub: many "alien" plants are not only garden staples, but also extremely well-behaved, and our landscapes would be immeasurably poorer without them. Imagine yourself bereft of your grandmother's favourite peony, your pristine stand of regal lilies, or even a couple of colourful autumn chrysanthemums, and you'll see that floral xenophobia is a slippery slope at best.

So why has the movement to exclude alien plants gained so much ground? Simply because so many of the introductions over the past few centuries have proven to be detrimental to natural ecosystems, not to mention being irksome to home gardeners. In fact, to try to establish a completely native plot is now very likely impossible, and if you attempt

What gardener could possibly deny permanent residency status to exotic aliens like bearded iris (Iris cvs.) and Oriental poppies (Papaver orientale)? As botanically courteous as any native species, these flowering plants should never be judged as good or bad based simply on their country of origin.

it, it will mean rooting out every dandelion (*Taraxacum officinale*), black medic (*Medicago lupulina*), and plantain (*Plantago spp.*) infestation from every inch of your soil. These aliens, coupled with our most recent blunder, purple loosestrife (*Lythrum salicaria*), have created a backlash against everything that is "non-native." Nevertheless, it's important to remember that plants have been travelling the globe since time began, often under their own steam, and they cannot be considered good or bad simply based on their country of origin. Whatever you do, don't become a flower fascist!

But if some plants are too aggressive, and others are too frail, what's left? Well, to be honest, it will depend where you live, and what your garden conditions will support most easily. For instance if you have an exposed site that's freezing cold in the winter and hellishly hot in summer, perhaps a prairie meadow would suit you best. On the other hand, if you inherit a property with mature trees that produce shady, dry zones, you will be more interested in woodland plants. Northern gardeners will likely be drawn to plants that display extreme hardiness in response to low temperatures, while gardeners in areas of high rainfall will want plants that tolerate damp surroundings and water-logged soil. Whatever your situation is across this massive and diverse country, there is a group of plants, both native and introduced, that will provide bloom, beauty, and sanctuary for wildlife around your home, and you won't have to give up your day job to look after them!

Creating a naturalized garden goes beyond just selecting the appropriate plants for specific conditions within your garden. In addition to being robust growers, it's important that they are also pest and disease free. For instance, there seems little point in growing native plants such as beebalm (*Monarda didyma*) and garden phlox (*Phlox paniculata*) if they are going to be covered in powdery mildew for much of the season. If a disease like this is prevalent in your area, it's well worth spending some extra time to search out mildew-resistant cultivars.

By the same token, many of our native evening primroses (*Oenothera spp.* and cvs.) are troubled by aphids. Rather than resorting to sprays (even organic ones), natural gardeners might attempt a different approach: perhaps the solution could be as simple as switching to a less susceptible species or cultivar within the genus; maybe the situation will be viewed as an opportunity to encourage beneficial insects such as ladybugs and lacewings into your garden (aphids are one of their primary food sources); or perhaps you'll decide to experiment with an altogether different plant family.

EXOTIC ALIENS THAT WE KNOW AND HATE
Black medic (*Medicago lupulina*) • Introduced from Eurasia as a fodder plant
Broad-leaved plantain (*Plantago major*) • Introduced (unintentionally) from Eurasia, it moved west with the settlers. Preferring compacted soil, it's also known as white-man's foot and cart-track plant.
Chickweed (*Stellaria media*) • Introduced from southern Europe
Common burdock (*Arctium minus*) • Introduced from Eurasia as a medicinal herb
Common mallow (*Malva neglecta*) • Introduced from Eurasia as a medical herb
Crabgrass (*Digitaria sanguinalis*) • Introduced from Europe for forage and hay
Dandelion (*Taraxacum officinale*) • Introduced from Eurasia as a salad green
Garlic mustard (*Alliaria petiolata*) • Introduced from Europe as a salad green
Purple loosestrife (*Lythrum salicaria*) • Introduced from Eurasia as an ornamental
Purslane (*Portulaca oleracea*) • Introduced from India as a salad green
Quackgrass (*Agropyron repens*) • Introduced from Eurasia
Yellow avens (*Geum aleppicum*) • Introduced from Eurasia

Plants such as hybrid tea roses, which suffer from both disease and insect pests, are best excluded from natural gardens, and their dependence on regular pruning, deadheading, and chemical fertilizers make them even less likely candidates for lower maintenance gardens. In spite of this, there are plenty of alternatives within the rose family: many old-fashioned and shrub roses won't expect you to pander to them, nor will the more recently introduced Agriculture Canada winter hardy roses (Explorer and Parkland series), so the choice appears to be self-evident.

In the best-case scenario, each plant will offer something to the garden, contributing to the ecosystem you are trying to create, rather than detracting from it. Trees and shrubs will provide food, shelter, and homes for many birds and small mammals, while flowering plants will lure butterflies, beneficial insects, pollinating bees, and even hummingbirds into your garden. Never lose sight of the fact that naturalized gardens work with nature — not against it — and that the principles of the naturalized gardening approach can be

applied to any setting. Without a doubt this will entail a certain amount of critical surveillance on the gardener's part, especially in the initial stages, but with experience, your scrutinizing skills will sharpen, and in any case, what gardener doesn't love to spend time inspecting their horticultural handiwork?

a pithy history of naturalized gardening

As King Solomon was wont to say, "The thing that hath been, it is that which shall be; and that which is done is that which shall be done: and there is no new thing under the sun" (Eccl. 1:9). Despite the advent of genetically modified organisms, I think that this statement is still a convincing one, and when it comes to naturalized gardening, it is very sound indeed. Like many of the gardening styles that North Americans espouse in the twenty-first century, naturalized gardening has its roots firmly fixed in the English countryside, and it is anything but new.

During the sixteenth and seventeenth centuries, most gardens in England reflected the older, more established garden designs that were popular in Europe. These Dutch, French, and Italian schemes emphasized geometric patterns in extremely formal layouts. We only have to picture a typical Elizabethan herb or "knot garden" to see how true this is — geometric rows of low, clipped hedges that contained the plants themselves, segregated from one another by strictly adhered-to boundaries that were maintained at all costs, or should I say, at great expense? Certainly, these designs required a multitude of labourers to keep their refined appearance intact. Rebellion seems intrinsic to human nature, so it's hardly surprising that by the eighteenth century, there was a backlash against these artificial "Spirograph" designs.

With the eighteenth century came a new romanticism, both in art and literature, and this fresh aesthetic was soon reflected in the landscape. Geometric designs were out, and parkland scenes were in. Suddenly everything from grand estates to local manor houses were being ensconced in sweeping, grassy pastures, with copses of trees and shrubs, artificial lakes and streams, and man-made hills and valleys. Local farmers and tenants weren't considered attractive enough to be included as constituents of this new bucolic representation and were relocated or evicted, only to be replaced by more efficient grassland grazers such as deer and sheep, who both manicured and fertilized the lawn at the same time.

Lancelot "Capability" Brown (1716–83) was in his element when it came to this kind of landscaping, and while in retrospect it's easy to be critical of some of his views, it's important to remember how revolutionary they were during his own lifetime. In the first

Legend has it that 'Rosa Mundi' (Rosa gallica versicolor) was named after Henry II's mistress, the "Fair Rosamund." An ancient strain, 'Rosa Mundi' isn't much bothered by insects or disease and is extremely hardy. Vita Suckville-West was enthusiastic: "Striped and splotched and blotted, this fine old rose explodes into fluorescence in June, giving endless variations of her markings."

PLANTS RECOMMENDED FOR NATURALIZED GARDENS (LATE 18TH CENTURY)

Columbine (*Aquilegia spp.*)

Cowslip (*Primula veris*)

Daffodils (*Narcissus spp.*)

Evening primrose (*Oenothera spp.*)

Honesty (*Lunaria spp.*)

Honeysuckle (*Lonicera spp.*)

Lavender (*Lavandula spp.*)

Lilies (*Lilium spp.*)

Marjoram (*Origanum majorana*)

Peonies (*Paeonia spp.*)

Primroses (*Primula vulgaris*)

Roses (*Rosa spp.*)

Scabious (*Knautia* and *Scabiosa spp.*)

Snowdrops (*Galanthus spp.*)

Spiraea (*Spiraea spp.*)

Sunflowers (*Helianthus spp.*)

Sweet William (*Dianthus barbatus*)

Violets (*Viola spp.*)

Wallflower (*Erysimum spp.*)

Woodland strawberry (*Fragaria vesca*)

place, he was always cognizant of the cultural requirements of the plants (mostly trees) he installed. Until then, the idea had been to select the plants most appropriate to the garden's overall design, but Brown turned this idea on its head and instead concentrated on plants that would thrive in the conditions on site.

Secondly, and perhaps more importantly, Brown's landscapes were without exception designed to reach fruition two hundred years hence, which shows great foresight on the landscaper's part and suggests tremendous patience on the homeowner's side. Fast-growing trees were planted to provide shelter and windbreaks for more permanent specimens, imitating (but not replicating) the natural progression of vegetation in the wild.

The son of a market gardener, and frequently cited as the most influential garden writer of the eighteenth century, Philip Miller (1691–1771) served as curator of the Chelsea Physic Garden in London from 1722 to 1770. During his lifetime he was universally known as the "Prince of Gardeners," but in the end he was dismissed from Chelsea for "obstinacy and impertinence" — at the age of seventy-nine. He wrote two important books: *The Gardeners Dictionary* (1731) ran to nine editions during his lifetime, and still serves as the prototype of all gardening dictionaries to this day, and *The Gardeners Kalendar* (1766).

In Miller's era, what we would call a naturalized garden was then referred to as a "wilderness." Many of the same methods that we use today to create a natural garden are clearly delineated in the 1754 edition of *The Gardeners Dictionary*: "Wildernesses if rightly situated, artfully contrived, and judiciously planted, are very great Ornaments to a fine Garden. These Parts of a Garden should, in great measure, be design'd from Nature, so whatever has the stiff Appearance of Art does by no means correspond therewith. In the general Design of the Wildernesses, it should not be studied to make the several Parts correspondent; for that is so formal and stiff, as to be now quite rejected: the greater Diversity there is in the Distribution of these Parts, the more Pleasure they will afford. In Wildernesses, there is but little Trouble or Expense after their first planting, which is an Addition to their Value." Sound familiar?

By the end of the eighteenth century, wealthy North Americans began to travel to Europe, and to England and France in particular. Impressed by the English parkland movement, and the French interpretation of it, called a *jardin anglais,* once home, they began to replicate these designs on their own estates. In particular, Thomas Jefferson often visited England during his tenure in Paris during the last half of the 1780s, and his exposure to the naturalized style of gardening was unquestionably reflected in his flower gardens at Monticello.

The next great proponent of the natural parkland style in North America was Frederick Law Olmstead (1822–98). Known best for immense projects like Mount Royal in Montreal and Central Park in New York City, he was one of the first landscape architects to introduce native plants on a grand scale. Although he candidly admitted that if all the topsoil he had added to the Central Park site was spread out evenly, it would be at least four feet high, he distributed it with skill, concocting small hills and valleys in much the same way that English landscapers had done a century before. He even gave instructions that herbaceous plants "should be introduced in patches and encouraged to completely cover the surface." This was a marked departure from what was going on in urban parks elsewhere across North America, where, for the most part, annual "carpet bedding" designs had come into vogue.

Olmstead admired and corresponded regularly with the famous Anglo-Irish gardener William Robinson (1838–1935). Robinson encouraged Olmstead's predilection toward a more natural style and also suggested that he include European plants as well as North American natives in his designs.

I'm certain that it's almost impossible to write a book about gardening without mentioning William Robinson at some point, since he was without a doubt a man ahead of his time, and much of what he wrote over one hundred and twenty-five years ago is still applicable today.

Born in Ireland, Robinson started out as a garden boy for the Marquis of Waterford at his Ballykilcannan estate, where he quickly rose to the position of foreman. After quarrelling with the Marquis, he left his post abruptly, but not before swinging open all the doors and windows of m'lord's tropical greenhouses on a particularly frosty evening — effectively wiping out an expensive collection of rare exotics. Incredibly, this massacre doesn't appear to have been a particularly career-damaging move, since shortly afterwards, he secured a position at the Royal Botanic Society's garden in London, where he began writing in the 1860s.

His first significant book, *The Wild Garden* (1870), which was subtitled *Our groves and shrubberies made beautiful by the naturalization of hardy exotic plants,* takes up nicely where Miller's earlier treatise on "wilderness" gardens left off. In *The Wild Garden,* Robinson promotes the idea of "placing plants of other countries, as hardy as our hardiest wildflowers, in places where they will flourish without further care or cost."

Using both native and introduced hardy perennial plants (instead of tender annuals) and placing them in situations where they would spread and multiply is a hallmark of the

Robinson style. He espoused installing plants in situations that matched as closely as possible their natural habitats, making him something of an ecologist before the phrase had even been coined.

Judiciously, Robinson also encouraged gardeners to become intimate with their own properties, a sentiment I heartily applaud. In his most important book, *The English Flower Garden* (1883), he writes, "I believe that the best results can only be got by the owner who knows and loves his ground. The great evil is the stereotyped plan." More important than a blueprint was to consider the garden and the plants within it as a whole, or as Robinson put it, "the picture before the frame." Moreover, Robinson maintained that when plants are sited correctly, they not only grow better, they also look better. Hear! Hear!

By the last quarter of the twentieth century, the naturalized gardening movement once again gathered steam. Concerns over the wholesale use of chemical pesticides and fertilizers became more widespread, and rectangular stretches of golf-course-quality front lawns began to take on a sinister demeanour. Incidents of groundwater contamination due to intensive agricultural practices only served to add fuel to the fire.

Gradually, gardeners across the continent began to seriously consider the effect they were having on their environment, and better yet, they began to question why they were spreading such massive amounts of expensive synthetic chemicals around their homes. Slowly, expectations were adjusted, and before long, a few weeds in the turfgrass didn't seem to be quite the catastrophe it would have been only a few years earlier.

It occurs to me that if we all were forced to live off our own land for a few years, or were told that our children would have to spend the first five years of their lives eating fruit and vegetables produced exclusively in our own backyards, our attitudes would shift overnight. That's the beauty of natural gardening — it encourages gardening habits that will sustain the health and productivity of your land — not poison it.

THE BIRTH OF ECOLOGY

Despite the fact that Ernst Haeckel came up with the word *oecologie* in 1866 (from the Greek *oikos*, referring to the household and its daily management), the idea of ecology was still unfamiliar to most people in the nineteenth century. Then, in 1895, a Danish professor, Eugenius Warming, wrote a paper entitled *The Oecology of Plants: An Introduction to the Study of Plant Communities*. By the turn of the century, botanists at the University of Chicago had jumped on the ecological bandwagon, along with Jens Jensen (1860–1951), an influential Danish landscape architect who worked in Chicago from 1884 to 1935. Jensen collaborated with architectural luminaries such as Frank Lloyd Wright and was responsible for incorporating many native plants into his designs at a time when few North American gardeners took their local flora seriously.

Interest in ecologically responsible gardening grew during the first part of the twentieth century, culminating in a book (recently reissued) called *American Plants for American Gardens* (1929). Unhappily, the publication of this book coincided with the stock market crash, followed by the Depression, followed by World War II. It wasn't until the 1960s that the ecology movement once more began to gain impetus, starting with Rachel Carson's book *Silent Spring* (1962), continuing on with Ian McHarg's *Design with Nature* (1966), and capped by the first Earth Day, held on April 22, 1970.

It is surely a scene like this that William Robinson had in mind when he subtitled his first important book (The Wild Garden) "Our groves and shrubberies made beautiful by the naturalization of hardy exotic plants."

Gardening by its very nature is half science, half art. "Getting things right" in the garden scientifically enables us to move on to the second, more important and fulfilling part, which is the individual gardener's freedom of expression. And even the courts are catching on! In 1996, a Toronto, Ontario, bylaw which "prohibited excessive growth of weeds and grass" on private property was struck down. The popular definition of a weed is simply "any plant growing where you don't want it to," but nevertheless, Judge David Fairgrieve ruled that the bylaw "imposed on all property owners the conventional landscaping practices considered by most people to be desirable, and [that] one of its effects is to prevent naturalized gardens which reflect other, less conventional attitudes." The future is looking rosier already!

Whether naturalized gardens represent less conventional attitudes is open to discussion, but most gardeners want to be creative, experimental, and, often, unconventional. In the next chapter we'll explore the ins and outs of creating and maintaining a naturalized garden, and how we can apply the lessons of pioneering natural gardeners like Brown, Miller, Olmstead, and Robinson to our own twenty-first-century Edens.

Many gardeners will want to include some vegetables in their naturalized garden, making it more important than ever to dispense with chemical pesticides. Once cool-season crops like lettuce (pictured here with yarrow [Achillea cvs.]) have been harvested, they can be replaced with warm-season vegetable transplants such as beans, tomatoes, and rutabagas.

getting started,
keeping going

*One of the first things for natural gardeners
to do will be to evaluate their property and
determine what sort of garden their land
can realistically and reasonably support.
Once you've decided on a particular garden
style, it's time to get creative!*

The first thing you'll have to decide before creating a naturalized garden is exactly where you stand — vegetatively speaking. That is, what gardening possibilities exist in your mind and on your site? What are your horticultural challenges? Visualizing what your "perfect" garden will look like is a good starting point. In this book, I'll examine the three dominant gardening avenues open to most of us to varying degrees: woodland gardens (part to full shade), natural meadows (part to full sun), and damp gardens.

Except for the prairies and the northern tundra, most of Canada and much of the United States were once either deciduous or (farther north and the Pacific Northwest) coniferous forest, but this doesn't mean you should confine yourself to only one branch of natural gardening. My garden has some areas that are best treated as woodland (shady and dry), and others that are low-lying and damp all year. Areas closer to the house tend to be sunny and dry (like a meadow), and since I always plant to encourage wildlife, I have ended up with a modest representation of the three gardening approaches within a fairly compact city garden. You can too!

Whether you concentrate on just one style of naturalized gardening or combine several is personal preference. You will have to think about how realistic a particular style is to your surroundings, but as far as aesthetics go, you're the boss! However, no matter what sort of garden you choose, there are a few guidelines every aspiring natural gardener needs to bear in mind.

hardiness zones

Like people, all gardens are imbued with an intrinsic potential, but they also usually include a number of impediments or limiting factors. The first of these limiting factors is temperature. All plants have a minimum and a maximum temperature restriction, below or above which they can't survive. Canada has been divided into ten hardiness zones, based primarily on minimum winter temperatures, with the warmest (Zone 9) occurring in a few spots of the Pacific Northwest, and the coldest (Zone 0) representing areas so far north that the potential for vegetation is negligible. The U.S. Department of Agriculture (USDA) and Agriculture Canada hardiness zones differ slightly, but usually only by a value of "one," so they are easy to convert. For example, a USDA Zone 5 is considered to be Zone 6 in Canada (add one); conversely, a Canadian Zone 8 would correspond with a USDA Zone 7 (subtract one). I use the Canadian system throughout this book.

Although gardeners can use plant hardiness zones as general perimeters, other influences such as altitude (average temperatures drop at higher elevations), the number of frost-free days in your region, the wind velocity, the amount of precipitation and humidity in your area, and particularly the maximum temperature in the summer, will all have a noticeable effect on the plants in your garden. It's also important to remember that most gardens have protected areas where "micro-climates" exist. For instance, a protected, sunny spot in a Zone 5 garden may well behave more like Zone 6 — exploit these distinct pockets in order to increase the range of plant material you are able to grow.

While it's often the case that a plant indigenous to a chilly Zone 2 region will be able to survive in a much warmer Zone 8 garden, the opposite is rarely true. Nonetheless, by experimenting with different plants, you will quickly get to know what works well in your garden, and what doesn't. I've been pleasantly surprised when plants such as the North African Byzantine gladiolus (*Gladiolus communis* subsp. *byzantinus*) or the South African summer hyacinth (*Galtonia candicans*), both reputedly hardy only to Zone 8, have returned for many years now in my Zone 6 garden. I accidentally discovered these extra-hardy characteristics when I forgot to lift and store the bulbs indoors one autumn. Experimentation (intentional or otherwise) is the key!

precipitation

Rainfall is the next issue to consider. If you live in an area with high rainfall, you'll want to seek out plants that don't mind getting their feet wet, and fortunately, there are a great many of these to choose from. At the other end of the spectrum, areas with low rainfall are best planted with deep-rooted, drought-tolerant plants, and again, gardeners are absolutely spoiled for choice.

Planting under mature trees is always something of a challenge, since these Goliaths inevitably produce dry, shady conditions beneath their magnificent canopies. The best solution for these problem areas is to plant deep-rooted (hence, drought-tolerant) shade-loving species such as hostas (Hosta cvs.), English ivy (Hedera helix) and lungwort (Pulmonaria cvs.).

DEEP-ROOTED NATIVE TREES AND SHRUBS

In the case of large, woody plant material, it's more important than ever to choose deep-rooted species if you suspect that adequate water may be a problem in some seasons. With their large, carrot-shaped taproots (often growing to a depth of over 4.5 m / 15 feet), these species are able to access groundwater, making them much less likely to be affected by drought or problems associated with surface soil compaction. Although trees and shrubs with taproots are sometimes difficult to transplant, once established, they won't interfere with septic tanks, wells, irrigation systems, or building foundations. Flowering plants are also easier to install under tap-rooted trees than beneath those with lateral surface roots.

TREES NAME	CULTIVATED SINCE	HARDY TO ZONE	TREES NAME	CULTIVATED SINCE	HARDY TO ZONE
Buckeye			Mockernut or White hickory (Carya tomentosa)	1766	5
Ohio buckeye (Aesculus glabra)	1809	4	Pecan (Carya illinoensis)	1760	6
Yellow buckeye (Aesculus flava)	1764	4	Pignut hickory (Carya glabra)	1750	5
			Shagbark hickory (Carya ovata)	1629	4
Hawthorn			**Oak**		
Cockspur hawthorn (Crataegus crusgalli)	1656	4	Blackjack oak (Quercus marilandica)	1739	5
Downy hawthorn (Crataegus mollis)	1683	3	Bur oak (Quercus macrocarpa)	1811	2
Glossy hawthorn (Crataegus nitida)	1883	5	Chestnut or Basket oak (Quercus prinus)	1688	5
Washington hawthorn (Crataegus phaenopyrum)	1738	5	Northern pin oak (Quercus ellipsoidalis)	1902	3
Thicket or Dotted hawthorn (Crataegus punctata)	1716	4	Post oak (Quercus stellata)	1819	4
			Scarlet oak (Quercus coccinea)	1691	5
Hickory			Shingle or Laurel oak (Quercus imbricaria)	1724	5
Bitternut hickory (Carya cordiformis)	1689	4			

Any newly installed garden will usually require some auxiliary water for the first two or three years while the plants become established, but after that, they're on their own, so it's important to choose species that will thrive in the conditions that your site (not you!) is able to provide. Remember that natural gardens are calculated to be low-maintenance gardens, and that homeowners shouldn't be expected to act as mobile cocktail lounges for their flowers.

If you must water your garden periodically to keep things going, some methods are far more efficient than others. Although sprinklers designed for irrigating lawns are a temptation to most gardeners, a better approach is to use drip or soaker hoses. With

DEEP-ROOTED NATIVE TREES AND SHRUBS (CONTINUED)

TREES NAME	CULTIVATED SINCE	HARDY TO ZONE	TREES NAME	CULTIVATED SINCE	HARDY TO ZONE
White oak (*Quercus alba*)	1724	4	Common sassafras (*Sassafras albidum*)	1630	5
Pine			Eastern redcedar (*Juniperus virginiana*)	1664	3
Limber pine (*Pinus flexilis*)	1852	2	Northern catalpa (*Catalpa speciosa*)	1754	5
Pitch pine (*Pinus rigida*)	1759	5	**SHRUBS**		
Ponderosa pine (*Pinus ponderosa*)	1827	3	**Juniper**		
Walnut			Common juniper (*Juniperus communis*)	n/a	2
Black walnut (*Juglans nigra*)	1686	4	Creeping juniper (*Juniperus horizontalis*)	1836	2
Butternut (*Juglans cinerea*)	1633	3	**Other Shrubs**		
Other Trees			Adam's-needle yucca (*Yucca filamentosa*)	1675	5
American sweetgum (*Liquidamber styraciflua*)	1681	6	Bristlecone pine (*Pinus aristata*)	1861	5
			Canadian yew (*Taxus canadensis*)	1800	2
Black gum (*Nyssa sylvatica*)	1750	5	Trailing arbutus (*Epigaea repens*)	1736	2

sprinklers, much of the water is lost to evaporation, and it also douses the plants themselves, a situation that can often lead to the proliferation of fungal and bacterial diseases. Ground-level soaker hoses keep plant foliage dry, they dispense water slowly so that it can be absorbed deeply and thoroughly, and little or nothing is lost to evaporation. And your well won't run dry.

mulches

Gardeners frequently apply commercially available mulches to the soil surface to conserve water while freshly installed plants become accustomed to their new surroundings, but after the first few years it's best to let nature do the mulching. Fallen leaves and other plant detritus will gradually be incorporated into the top layers of the soil, where they will break down at a leisurely pace, releasing nutrients while simultaneously improving the texture of the soil. Fallen leaves represent a considerable share of the garden's overall bounty — an annual dividend that is often overlooked.

In areas where rainfall is low or undependable, it's important to choose drought-tolerant perennials such as beebalm (Monarda didyma and cvs.), the flower that's responsible for the distinctive flavour of Earl Grey tea. A plant that was once a martyr to powdery mildew, beebalm has several mildew-resistant cultivars that are now on the market.

Inorganic mulches such as gravel or marble chips are expensive, and in any case they look too formal in a naturalized setting. Nor would I recommend organic mulches such as peat moss or salt marsh hay since both are harvested from endangered wetland habitats.

Commercial mulches also represent a bit of a double-edged sword: To their credit, they conserve water and prevent many of the more exasperating weed seeds from germinating. On the other hand, they also prevent the germination of seeds from desirable plants, many of which will have been installed expressly for the purpose of spreading about the garden in a natural fashion. North Americans tend to be very tidy gardeners, a fact brought home rather forcibly when I was in England recently.

While I was visiting some of "The Great Gardens," it was all I could do to keep my secateurs in my pocket — there were maturing seed heads everywhere! I commented on this to one of my hosts, who replied, "Yes, that's how this old garden regenerates itself." And I soon saw that this was the case — everywhere noble stands of Bulgarian allium

(*Necteroscordum siculum* [syn. *Allium bulgaricum*]) had scattered themselves around the garden, and I even found myself admiring their rocket-shaped ivory seed heads. Hardy geraniums (*Geranium* spp.) ran riot, and eventually I finished off by losing my heart to self-seeded mounds of golden spurge (*Euphorbia characias* 'Lambrook Gold'). I resolved then and there that I would be less meticulous about deadheading in the future!

If you do decide to use a thick bark or wood chip-based mulch when you install new plants, it's a good idea to add a plentiful source of nitrogen at the same time (a light sprinkling of blood meal or an occasional shower of diluted urine will both work well). Additional nitrogen is required since as the woody mulch decays, it robs the soil of much of its available nitrogen in the process. As a rule, apply blood meal at half the manufacturer's recommended rate — you can always add more later. Both blood meal and urine have the added benefit of discouraging neighbourhood dogs and cats from feeling one hundred percent at ease in your garden.

soil

Unquestionably, one of the most important factors in any garden is the soil. Being a good gardener above ground will always require a certain amount of attention and vigilance to what's going on below ground!

When a garden is first created, or when a mature garden is renovated, it isn't unusual to see dump trucks unloading topsoil, which is then spread willy-nilly around the property. While this approach will afford a quick fix for more conventional garden styles, it really isn't appropriate to the naturalized garden. What we're after is a long-term, sustainable game plan, which means that the plants you are able to grow successfully will depend largely on the original, unadulterated soil that's native to your area. In a natural garden, it's fine to improve and even to amend your soil, but it isn't at all a sound plan to attempt to change its essential character.

Local soils can have vastly different qualities within a fairly short distance. While I battle with sticky, compacted clay, less than two kilometres away, my colleagues are energetically bewailing their nutrient-deprived, quick-draining sandy soils. All the more reason to remember what William Robinson advised about knowing and loving your ground. The problem may not be so much with your soil, as with your unreasonable expectations of what it can realistically support.

Clay soils are made up of very small particles, which is why they tend to be compacted, wet, and slow to warm up in spring. Fortunately, they're rich in the essential nutrients and minerals that most plants require for healthy growth. Sandy soils have

very large particles (terrestrially speaking) and provide good drainage, but are usually low in nutrients. Soils with particle sizes in between these two extremes are known as silt.

Whether you find yourself dealing with clay, sand, or something betwixt the two, there is a surefire way to get more out of your soil, and that's by adding organic matter. All soils are primarily made up of weathered parent rock, but regardless of whether you begin with granite, quartz, shale, or limestone, fully one-third of your topsoil should be composed of organic matter and humus (decomposed organic matter).

Compost is the most celebrated and well-known source of organic matter, but it is by no means the only one. Fallen leaves, which eventually transform themselves into coveted, nutrient-rich leaf mould, is how Mother Nature manages the equation over the long term in most regions of North America, assisted by the millions of worms and microscopic organisms that healthy soil possesses. These selfless critters diligently break organic matter down, making it progressively available to the plants, while at the same time improving the texture (or tilth) of the soil.

In any case, the bottom line will always be the same: Despite your best efforts at improving the soil, in the case of large plants (and trees in particular), the root systems will always eventually penetrate beyond your carefully amended planting holes, and it is this unamended soil on which they will depend for their sustenance over their life span. This is one reason why Capability Brown's landscapes have lasted for hundreds of years — he planted long-lived specimens that he knew were well suited to the native soil in the areas where he installed them, and they have stood the test of time as a result. Since we've already established that natural gardeners don't have time to mollycoddle their plants, selecting suitable varieties in the first place becomes more critical than ever.

When you're selecting woody plant material for the naturalized garden, it's essential that you bear in mind the characteristics of your native soil. Regardless of how carefully you prepare planting holes, the roots of large specimens will always wander well beyond your carefully amended boundaries. Trees and shrubs should always be chosen according to their compatibility with your existing soil conditions.

pH

In addition to determining the particle size of your native soil (from clay to sand), the parent rock material in your area also influences your soil's pH, that is, whether it is acidic, neutral, or alkaline. The pH (from the French *pouvoir hydrogène,* or hydrogen power) scale measures the acidity or alkalinity of a substance from 0 (purely acidic) to 14 (purely basic or alkaline) with 7 as a neutral point.

Generally speaking, most of the garden plants that North Americans cultivate do best at a pH of about 6.5 or very slightly acidic. Strongly acidic soils (pH 4.0 to 5.0) often contain high concentrations of aluminum and manganese, both of which can prove toxic to many plants, but it is ideal for rhododendrons, azaleas, blueberries, heathers, and many coniferous trees and shrubs. Highly alkaline soils tend to suppress the

LONGEST-LIVED NATIVE TREES AND SHRUBS

If, like Capability Brown, you are planting with an eye to the future, then selecting long-lived woody plants becomes an important consideration. The following native tree species will hit their prime at about two hundred years of age. In other words, if you are currently between the ages of thirty and fifty, the seedling that you plant now will still be casting shade on your great-great-great-great-great-grandchildren. Now that's thrilling!

TREES (+200 YEARS) NAME	GROWTH RATE	HARDY TO ZONE
Fir		
Alpine fir (*Abies lasiocarpa*)	slow-medium	2
White fir (*Abies concolor*)	slow	4
Hickory		
Bitternut hickory (*Carya cordiformis*)	slow	4
Mockernut or White hickory (*Carya tomentosa*)	slow	5
Pecan (*Carya illinoensis*)	slow	6
Pignut hickory (*Carya glabra*)	slow	5
Shagbark hickory (*Carya ovata*)	slow	4
Oak		
Blackjack oak (*Quercus marilandica*)	slow	5
Bur oak (*Quercus macrocarpa*)	slow	2
Chinkapin oak (*Quercus muhlenbergi*)	slow	4
Northern pin oak (*Quercus ellipsoidalis*)	slow	3
Northern red oak (*Quercus borealis*)	medium	3

TREES (+200 YEARS) NAME	GROWTH RATE	HARDY TO ZONE
Post oak (*Quercus stellata*)	slow	5
Scarlet oak (*Quercus coccinea*)	medium-fast	5
Shingle oak (*Quercus imbricaria*)	slow	5
White oak (*Quercus alba*)	slow	4
Pine		
Eastern white pine (*Pinus strobus*)	medium	3
Limber pine (*Pinus flexilis*)	slow	2
Red pine (*Pinus resinosa*)	medium	2
Spruce		
Black Hills white spruce (*Picea glauca densata*)	slow	2
Colorado spruce (*Picea pungens*)	slow	2
Engelmann spruce (*Picea engelmanni*)	slow	2
White spruce (*Picea glauca*)	slow-medium	2
Other Trees		
American beech (*Fagus grandiflora*)	slow	3
American planetree (*Platanus occidentalis*)	fast	4

LONGEST-LIVED NATIVE TREES AND SHRUBS (CONTINUED)

TREES (+200 YEARS) NAME	GROWTH RATE	HARDY TO ZONE
American sweetgum (*Liquidamber styraciflua*)	slow-medium	6
Black walnut (*Juglans nigra*)	fast	4
Canada hemlock (*Tsuga canadensis*)	slow-medium	3
Common baldcypress (*Taxodium disticum*)	medium	5
Common Douglasfir (*Pseudotsuga taxifolia*)	medium	5
Common hackberry (*Celtis occidentalis*)	medium	3
Eastern arborvitae (*Thuja occidentalis*)	medium-fast	2
Eastern redcedar (*Juniperus virginiana*)	slow	3
Osageorange (*Maclura pomifera*)	fast	5

SHRUBS (+100 YEARS)

Holly

NAME	GROWTH RATE	HARDY TO ZONE
Possumhaw (*Ilex decidua*)	slow-medium	5
Inkberry (*Ilex glabra*)	slow	4

SHRUBS (+100 YEARS) NAME	GROWTH RATE	HARDY TO ZONE
Juniper		
Common juniper (*Juniperus communis*)	slow	2
Creeping juniper (*Juniperus horizontalis*)	slow	2
Oak		
Scrub oak (*Quercus ilicifolia*)	medium	5
Dwarf Chinkapin oak (*Quercus prinoides*)	slow	5
Other Shrubs		
Bearberry (*Arctostaphylos uva-ursi*)	slow	2
Bristlecone pine (*Pinus aristata*)	slow	5
Bunchberry dogwood (*Cornus canadensis*)	slow	2
Canada yew (*Taxus canadensis*)	slow	2
Silver buffaloberry (*Shepherdia argentea*)	medium	2
Silverberry (*Eleagnus commutata*)	fast	2
Wintergreen (*Gaultheria procumbens*)	slow	3

NATIVE TREES AND SHRUBS THAT ARE TOLERANT OF STRONGLY ACIDIC SOILS (pH 4.0–5.0)

TREES NAME	pH RANGE	HARDY TO ZONE
Birch		
Sweet birch (*Betula lenta*)	4.5–5.0	3
Yellow birch (*Betula lutea*)	4.5–8.0	3
River birch (*Betula nigra*)	4.0–6.5	5
Fir		
Alpine fir (*Abies lasiocarpa*)	4.0–6.5	2
Balsam fir (*Abies balsamea*)	4.0–6.5	2
White fir (*Abies concolor*)	4.0–6.5	4
Maple		
Mountain maple (*Acer spicatum*)	4.0–5.0	2
Striped maple (*Acer pensylvanicum*)	4.0–5.0	3
Oak		
Blackjack oak (*Quercus marilandica*)	4.5–5.0	5
Bur oak (*Quercus macrocarpa*)	4.5–8.0	2
Post oak (*Quercus stellata*)	4.5–6.5	5
Shingle oak (*Quercus imbricaria*)	4.5–6.0	5
Pine		
Eastern white pine (*Pinus strobus*)	4.5–6.5	3
Jack pine (*Pinus banksiana*)	4.5–6.5	2
Limber pine (*Pinus flexilis*)	4.5–6.5	2
Red pine (*Pinus resinosa*)	4.5–6.5	2
Spruce		
Black spruce (*Picea mariana*)	4.5–6.5	2
Colorado spruce (*Picea pungens*)	4.5–6.5	2

TREES NAME	pH RANGE	HARDY TO ZONE
Engelmann spruce (*Picea engelmanni*)	4.5–6.5	2
White spruce (*Picea glauca*)	4.5–8.0	2
Other Trees		
American chestnut (*Castanea dentata*)	4.0–6.0	5
Black ash (*Fraxinus nigra*)	4.5–6.5	2
Canada hemlock (*Tsuga canadensis*)	4.5–6.5	3
Carolina silverbell (*Halesia carolina*)	4.5–6.0	5
Cucumbertree magnolia (*Magnolia acuminata*)	4.5–7.0	5
Franklin tree (*Franklinia alatamaha*)	4.5–6.0	6
White fringetree (*Chionanthus virginicus*)	4.5–6.5	5
SHRUBS		
Blueberry		
Cranberry (*Vaccinium macrocarpum*)	4.0–6.0	3
Highbush blueberry (*Vaccinium corymbosum*)	3.5–6.5	4
Lowbush blueberry (*Vaccinium angustifolium*)	4.0–6.0	2
Ceanothus		
Inland ceanothus (*Ceanothus ovatus*)	4.5–6.0	3
Jerseytea ceanothus (*Ceanothus americanus*)	4.5–6.0	3
Clethra		
Cinnamon clethra (*Clethra acuminata*)	4.5–6.5	6

NATIVE TREES AND SHRUBS THAT ARE TOLERANT OF STRONGLY ACIDIC SOILS (pH 4.0–5.0) (CON'T)

SHRUBS NAME	pH RANGE	HARDY TO ZONE	SHRUBS NAME	pH RANGE	HARDY TO ZONE
Summersweet clethra (*Clethra alnifolia*)	4.5–6.5	4	Bearberry (*Arctostaphylos uva-ursi*)	4.5–6.0	2
Holly			Blackcap raspberry (*Rubus occidentalis*)	4.5–6.5	4
Common winterberry (*Ilex verticillata*)	4.5–8.0	3	Bogrosemary andromeda (*Andromeda polifolia*)	4.0–6.0	2
Inkberry (*Ilex glabra*)	4.5–6.0	4			
Possumhaw (*Ilex decidua*)	4.0–8.5	5	Box sandmyrtle (*Leiophyllum buxifolium*)	4.0–6.0	6
Kalmia			Bunchberry dogwood (*Cornus canadensis*)	4.5–6.0	2
Bog kalmia (*Kalmia polifolia*)	4.0–5.5	2			
Mountainlaurel kalmia (*Kalmia latifolia*)	4.5–6.0	5	He-huckleberry (*Lyonia ligustrina*)	4.0–6.0	5
Rhododendron			Labradortea ledum (*Ledum groenlandicum*)	3.0–5.5	2
Sweet azalea (*Rhododendron arborescens*)	4.5–6.0	4			
Swamp azalea (*Rhododendron viscosum*)	4.0–6.0	4	Mountain pieris (*Pieris floribunda*)	4.5–6.0	5
Other Shrubs			Trailing arbutus (*Epigaea repens*)	4.5–6.0	2
Allegheny blackberry (*Rubus allegheniensis*)	4.5–7.5	3	Wintergreen (*Gaultheria procumbens*)	4.5–6.5	3
			Yellowroot (*Xanthorhiza simplicissima*)	4.0–6.5	5

Carolina silverbell (Halesia carolina syn. H. tetraptera) is one of my favourite native trees, but sadly, it is rarely encountered in home gardens. Hardy to Zones 4 to 5, and exceptionally pest resistant, silverbells prefer acidic soil conditions (pH 4.5 to 6.0). Keep an eye out for some of the newer cultivars such as 'Arnold Pink', 'Variegata', and 'Wedding Bells'.

Well suited to a naturalized setting, our native Eastern redbud (Cercis canadensis) favours an alkaline soil (pH 6.0 to 8.0) and is hardy to Zones 4 to 5. I grew up with the Eurasian Judas-tree (Cercis siliquastrum), but find the Eastern redbud unique in that it always produces its flowers before its leaves emerge. The purple-leaved cultivar 'Forest Pansy' is especially choice.

NATIVE TREES AND SHRUBS THAT ARE TOLERANT OF ALKALINE SOILS (pH 7.5–8.5)

TREES NAME	pH RANGE	HARDY TO ZONE
Hawthorn		
Cockspur hawthorn (*Crataegus crusgalli*)	6.0–8.0	4
Dotted hawthorn (*Crataegus punctata*)	6.0-8.0	4
Downy hawthorn (*Crataegus mollis*)	6.0–8.0	3
Glossy hawthorn (*Crataegus nitida*)	6.0–8.0	5
Washington hawthorn (*Crataegus phaenopyrum*)	6.0–8.0	5
Oak		
Bur oak (*Quercus macrocarpa*)	4.5–8.0	2
Chinkapin oak (*Quercus muhlenbergi*)	6.5–8.0	4
Walnut		
Butternut (*Juglans cinerea*)	6.5–8.0	3
Black walnut (*Juglans nigra*)	6.5–8.0	4
Viburnum		
Blackhaw viburnum (*Viburnum prunifolium*)	6.5–8.0	3
Nannyberry viburnum (*Viburnum lentago*)	6.0–7.5	2
Other Trees		
American elm (*Ulmus americana*)	6.5–8.0	2
American hophornbeam (*Ostrya virginiana*)	6.0–8.0	5
American planetree (*Platanus occidentalis*)	6.5–8.0	4
American smoketree (*Cotinus americanus*)	6.5–8.0	6
American yellowwood (*Cladrastis lutea*)	6.5–8.0	3
Bitternut hickory (*Carya cordiformis*)	5.5–8.0	4
Black locust (*Robinia pseudoacacia*)	5.0–7.5	3

NATIVE TREES AND SHRUBS THAT ARE TOLERANT OF ALKALINE SOILS (pH 7.5–8.5) (CONTINUED)

TREES NAME	pH RANGE	HARDY TO ZONE	SHRUBS NAME	pH RANGE	HARDY TO ZONE
Blue ash (*Fraxinus quadrangulata*)	6.5–8.0	5	**Juniper**		
Common hackberry (*Celtis occidentalis*)	6.5–8.0	3	Common juniper (*Juniperus communis*)	5.0–8.5	2
Common pawpaw (*Asimia triloba*)	6.0–8.0	5	Creeping juniper (*Juniperus horizontalis*)	5.0–8.5	2
Eastern arborvitae (*Thuja occidentalis*)	6.0–8.0	2	**Snowberry**		
Eastern red cedar (*Juniperus virginiana*)	6.0–8.0	3	Common snowberry (*Symphoricarpos albus*)	6.0–8.5	2
Eastern redbud (*Cercis canadensis*)	6.0–8.0	5	Western snowberry (*Symphoricarpos occidentalis*)	5.5–8.5	2
Northern catalpa (*Catalpa speciosa*)	6.0–8.0	5	**Other Shrubs**		
Osageorange (*Maclura pomifera*)	6.0–8.0	5	Bush cinquefoil (*Potentilla fruticosa*)	6.0–8.5	2
Paper birch (*Betula papyrifera*)	5.0–8.0	2	Clove currant (*Ribes odoratum*)	6.0–8.5	3
Red mulberry (*Morus rubra*)	6.5–8.0	5	Common buttonbush (*Cephalanthus occidentalis*)	6.0–8.5	4
SHRUBS			Common ninebark (*Physocarpus opulifolius*)	6.0–8.5	2
Amorpha			Corymed spirea (*Spiraea corymbosa*)	6.0–8.5	5
Indigobush amorpha (*Amorpha fruticosa*)	6.0–8.5	3	Dwarf Chinkapin oak (*Quercus prinoides*)	5.0–8.5	5
Leadplant amorpha (*Amorpha canescens*)	7.0–8.5	3	Fragrant sumac (*Rhus aromatica*)	6.0–8.5	4
Buffaloberry			Low birch (*Betula pumila*)	5.0–8.5	2
Russet buffaloberry (*Shepherdia canadensis*)	6.0–8.5	2	Mockorange (*Philadelphus grandiflorus*)	6.0–8.5	6
Silver buffaloberry (*Shepherdia argentea*)	6.0–8.5	2	Oregon grape (*Mahonia aquifolium*)	5.0–8.5	5
Dogwood			Rafinesque viburnum (*Viburnum rafinesquianum*)	6.0–8.5	3
Gray dogwood (*Cornus racemosa*)	6.0–8.5	3	Roseacacia locust (*Robinia hispida*)	6.0–8.5	4
Redosier dogwood (*Cornus stolonifera*)	6.0–8.5	2	Roseshell azalea (*Rhododendron roseum*)	5.0–8.0	4
Roundleaf dogwood (*Cornus rugosa*)	6.0–8.5	3	Roundleaf serviceberry (*Amelanchier sanguinea*)	6.0–8.5	5
Hydrangea			Scarlet elder (*Sambucus pubens*)	6.0–8.5	3
Oakleaf hydrangea (*Hydrangea quercifolia*)	6.0–8.5	6	Silverberry (*Elaeagnus commutata*)	6.0–8.5	2
Smooth hydrangea (*Hydrangea arborescens*)	6.0–8.5	4			

availability of essential soil micronutrients (especially iron, zinc, and copper), but on the other hand, they are usually teeming with beneficial micro-organisms.

It isn't difficult to determine your soil's pH. Inexpensive kits are available at most garden centres and nurseries, but if you would like a more accurate analysis, contact the local branch of your provincial Ministry of Agriculture and Food or State Department of Agriculture. Once you have your results, take them to heart. Trying to make alkaline soil acidic, or acidic soil alkaline, is against all the principles of natural gardening. The trick here is to work with what you have, and to make the most of it. Inevitably you will covet what you don't possess — the grass really is always greener on the other side!

Comfort yourself in the fact you'll find yourself in good company: Countless revered garden writers from Margery Fish (1892–1969) to Beverley Nichols (1898–1983) have cultivated fabulous gardens on alkaline soils, while at the same time (in print, at least) lusting after the more acidic conditions that would have enabled them to cultivate cherished calcifuges (acid-loving plants) like heaths and heathers (*Erica spp.*), mountain laurels (*Kalmia latifolia*), azaleas and rhododendrons (*Rhododendron spp.*). But when all was said and done, they invariably created their masterpieces using the tools they had at hand. So can you.

designing the naturalized garden

Far be it from me to tell you how to design your naturalized garden, or what it should look like when it's completed. That would be presumptuous in the extreme. Every individual's garden should reflect that person's particular style and flair. By being true to yourself and your own tastes, you will inevitably create an outdoor space that satisfies you both creatively and environmentally. No one else can do this for you. If you remember what Philip Miller said about the garden looking as if it had been "design'd from Nature," and his warning to reject stiff formality in favour of diversity and an unrestrained, natural approach, you won't go far wrong. Let his admonition be your guiding light.

NATIVE VINES FOR NATURALIZED GARDENS

Although more closely associated with woodland and damp gardens, native vines also can make a valuable contribution to meadow gardens. Providing an important food source for wildlife, they also add an undeniable rhythm and grace to naturalized settings.

NAME	HARDY TO ZONE	WILDLIFE VALUE
Clematis		
Rock clematis (*Clematis verticillaris*)	2	Songbirds (leaves poisonous)
Virgin's bower (*Clematis virginiana*)	3	Songbirds (leaves poisonous)
Grape		
Fox grape (*Vitis labrusca*)	4	Songbirds, waterfowl, mammals
Riverbank grape (*Vitis riparia*)	2	Songbirds, gamebirds, waterfowl
Honeysuckle		
Limber honeysuckle (*Lonicera dioica*)	2	Songbirds, gamebirds
Trumpet honeysuckle (*Lonicera sempervirens*)	4	Gamebirds, small mammals
Other Vines		
American bittersweet (*Celastrus scandens*)	2	Songbirds, small mammals
Bamboo greenbrier (*Smilax tamnoides*)	3	Winter songbirds, wood ducks
Crossvine (*Bignonia capreolata*)	6	Attracts hummingbirds
Dutchman's pipe (*Aristolochia durior*)	4	Valued for cover and nesting
Heartleaf ampelopsis (*Ampelopsis cordata*)	5	Songbirds, gamebirds
Kentucky wisteria (*Wisteria macrostachya*)	5	Low, poisonous fruits
Moonseed (*Menispermum canadense*)	2	Many birds and mammals
Trumpet vine (*Campsis radicans*)	5	Attracts hummingbirds
Virginia creeper (*Parthenocissus quinquefolia*)	2	High, primarily songbirds

Since mimicking nature is the order of the day, there are a few principles that will help you achieve a natural look, even while your plantings are becoming established. In nature, plants grow in groups (think of them as plant communities). These groups usually contain some representatives from the woody plant group (trees, shrubs, and

NON-NATIVE VINES FOR NATURALIZED GARDENS

Several well-behaved "alien" vines are also eminently suited to the naturalized garden. Some are remarkable for their fragrant flowers, while others furnish colourful foliage throughout the growing season. Most flowering vines require several hours of sunlight per day.

COMMON AND BOTANICAL NAMES	NATIVE TO	ZONES	EXPOSURE
Chinese wisteria (*Wisteria sinensis* and cultivars)	China	5 to 8	Sun/part sun
Climbing hydrangea (*Hydrangea petiolaris*)	Russia, Japan	4 to 9	Sun/part sun
English ivy (*Hedera helix* and cultivars)	Europe	5 to 10	Shade
Five-leaved akebia (*Akebia quinata* 'Variegata')	China, Japan	4 to 9	Sun/part shade
Golden hops (*Humulus lupulus* 'Aureus')	Eurasia, N. America	4 to 8	Sun/part shade
Japanese wisteria (*Wisteria floribunda* and cultivars)	Japan	5 to 9	Sun/part sun
Perennial sweet pea (*Lathyrus latifolius* 'White Pearl')	S. Europe	5 to 9	Sun/part sun
Porcelain berry (*Ampelopsis brevipedunculata* 'Elegans')	N.E. Asia	5 to 8	Sun/part sun
Variegated kiwi (*Actinidia kolomikta* 'Arctic Beauty')	E. Asia	4 to 9	Sun

roses) as well as from the herbaceous plant group (flowers and bulbs, grasses and herbs), making for a fairly cosmopolitan mixture. In naturalized gardens, trees, shrubs, and flowers are grouped together, but then these groups are grouped into groups! These combinations shouldn't end up looking like a horticultural mish-mash: Instead, the groupings should seem like a seamless succession of plants — different heights, different forms, and different seasons of bloom, all enjoying the same conditions, and all working together to form a cohesive tapestry. As the garden matures, the tapestry will alter, but if it is planted with a view to the future, it will always be beautiful.

existing features

Whether you are starting from scratch, or are converting an existing garden to a more naturalized style, you will inevitably come up against a few issues that will need addressing. Existing "hardscape" features like driveways, paths, and walls are facts of life and must be integrated into the garden plan while at the same time maintaining their utilitarian functions.

Native from Russia to Japan and not introduced to the west until 1865, climbing hydrangea (Hydrangea petiolaris syn. H. anomala subsp. petiolaris) has quickly gained celebrity status, so much so that woody plant authority Michael Dirr has dubbed it "the best vine!" Taking several years to establish, it matures into a vigorous climber, capable of swallowing up municipal signage in a single gulp.

A simple solution for maintaining your privacy is to plant trees and large shrubs on the periphery of your property, and then gradually decrease the scale as you get closer to your house. This approach ensures that plenty of space will be left for sun-loving perennials.

The easiest way to soften these hard edges is to insinuate plants along their borders — groundcovers and vines work well, and before long you'll find some perennials creeping into the picture. I have self-seeded Michaelmas daisies (*Aster novi-belgii*), columbines (*Aquilegia* 'McKana Hybrids'), golden fumitory (*Corydalis lutea*), and Argentinean verbena (*Verbena bonariensis*) adorning the cracks in my driveway, and strangely enough, they seem to grow better in these seemingly hostile conditions than they do in the garden proper.

Some gardens will have charming views that deserve to be framed (arbours, trellises, trees, and shrubs are the best way to go), but many of us are more concerned with blocking views, especially those of us who live in urban centres. If this is the case where you live, a good approach is to plant large woody plant material (trees and large shrubs) on the peripheries of your property, and then to gradually decrease the scale as you get closer to your house (flowers, herbs, bulbs, and small shrubs). This is an effective method of maintaining your privacy without sacrificing the opportunity to grow plants that require sunny conditions.

Many established gardens will also contain large, mature trees, and often they aren't varieties that we would have chosen ourselves. My back garden is dominated by a fifty-year-old Norway maple (*Acer platanoides* 'Crimson King'), and although I find its dense shade troublesome, its thick, waxy leaves useless for mulching, its invasive lateral root system overwhelming, and its unwanted seedlings too numerous, it remains an immutable fact of my gardening life. Oh, what I wouldn't give for a long-lived, taprooted oak (*Quercus spp.*)! What were they thinking?

In addition to its being illegal in many areas, tree removal is an expensive, messy process, and since you'll likely be left dealing with both stumps and immense roots for years to come, it's generally prudent to just accept your situation and to make the best of it. Pruning out lower branches (or "limbing up") will increase air circulation and light penetration at ground level, and choosing plant material that will tolerate the dry, shady conditions beneath mature tree canopies will ultimately provide the most practical solution.

Having evaluated your plot, making note of exposure, soil conditions, moisture and light levels, and areas that require blocking or framing, you are now ready to start mapping out the style or styles of natural garden you would like to create on your property. Always bear in mind which plants will work best in each location.

If (like me) you would like a bit of everything, think about what style will work best in what area of your garden. Remember, if you already have some mature trees on your lot, perhaps this is the spot for a woodland area; dry, sunny areas will be suitable for a small prairie meadow; and low-lying areas that collect water will provide a suitable site for a damp garden. By choosing plants that provide both food and shelter for insects and animals, you will simultaneously create pockets where sustainable, natural habitats will be the primary focus.

In the following chapters, we will concentrate on some of the best plant choices for each of these naturalized garden styles. Once you have studied and compared these plant portraits, you'll be ready for one of the most enjoyable of all gardening pursuits: composing the short list preparatory to your next trip to the nursery or garden centre!

the woodland garden

There is no dearth of flowers in the woodland garden during the spring, before deciduous tree leaves unfold and block out much of the sunlight. Pictured here, at the foot of several white birch trees (Betula papyrifera) are drifts of (background) Japanese spurge (Pachysandra terminalis) and (foreground) periwinkle (Vinca minor), which are in turn punctuated by the brilliant red of several Fosteriana tulips (Tulipa 'Madame Lefeber' syn. 'Red Emperor').

Of all the natural gardening styles, the woodland and woodland margin garden remains one of the most popular. Its trees lend a sense of permanency and privacy, its flowering shrubs fill in the nooks and crannies, and its springtime floral display is no less brilliant than the gaudy hues of its autumn foliage.

In fact, I think that many gardeners subconsciously adopt the woodland garden style due to its wonderful ability to delineate the passage of time as precisely as it does. From the stark architecture of its winter branches to the first swelling of leaf and flower buds, the woodland garden anticipates the passing seasons more eloquently than any other.

Woodland gardens are also closely associated with a thriving wildlife community, and with good reason. Trees and shrubs provide innumerable nesting sites and hiding places for all manner of beasts, from lowly insects and reptiles to the birds and small mammals that we have come to associate with a well-balanced ecosystem. The leaves, fruit, and nuts that woodland plants furnish represent a vital food source for these same deserving creatures.

Having decided where the woodland section of your garden is to be situated (northern exposures work well), and having assessed your soil and site conditions, it's now time to start "preparing the area," as surgeons are so fond of saying. This will entail removing invasive and exotic species that you don't wish to include, as well as giving the soil a bit of a pre-planting boost.

Now is the perfect time to augment your layer of organic matter and leaf mould by incorporating additional shredded leaves into the top layers of the soil profile. Give nature a hand by shredding the leaves before mixing them into the soil — this will help to speed up their decomposition immeasurably, transforming them into an immediately effective natural mulch and soil conditioner. If you don't own a leaf shredder, throwing a basket of dry leaves (I consider oak leaves to be the *crème de la crème* for this purpose) into a metal garbage can and letting loose with a weed whacker will certainly do the trick. Spreading dried leaves on your lawn and then passing over them several times with a lawn mower will also produce the desired results. Adding a little blood and bone meal (good sources of nitrogen and phosphorus, respectively) is also a sound idea at this juncture.

The best time for planting a woodland garden is either early spring or late fall (I prefer the latter). Contrary to popular opinion, the root growth of most woody plants takes place when soil temperatures are cool (spring and autumn). When the ground temperatures are extremely hot (summer) or cold (winter) roots maintain a "holding pattern" and don't grow at all. This is why woody material is often planted when it's dormant, and an easy way to picture this is if we consider the practice of planting roses bare-root.

THE CARBON:NITROGEN RATIO

In order for leaves to decompose into leaf mould, the carbon that is stored within each leaf must be broken down by soil micro-organisms that are in turn fuelled by nitrogen. This explains why leaves decay more quickly in moist, nitrogen-rich topsoil than they do on very dry, nutrient-poor sandy soils. Leaves also vary widely in the amount of carbon they contain, and this is expressed as the C:N (or "carbon to nitrogen") ratio. For instance, leaves with a high C:N ratio (e.g., larch) will break down slowly due to their high carbon content, while leaves with a low carbon content (e.g., alder) will break down much more quickly. Adding a good source of nitrogen such as blood meal, worm castings, or composted manure to your shredded leaves will speed up the decomposition process considerably, rendering them efficacious to plants sooner rather than later. Here are some examples of the C:N ratio of common tree leaves:

Alder (*Alnus spp.*)	15:1	Larch (*Larix spp.*)	113:1
Ash (*Fraxinus spp.*)	21:1	Linden (*Tilia spp.*)	37:1
Aspen (*Populus spp.*)	63:1	Maple (*Acer spp.*)	52:1
Beech (*Fagus spp.*)	51:1	Oak (*Quercus spp.*)	47:1
Birch (*Betula spp.*)	50:1	Pine (*Pinus spp.*)	66:1
Black elder (*Sambucus spp.*)	22:1	Red oak (*Quercus rubra*)	53:1
Elm (*Ulmus spp.*)	28:1	Spruce (*Picea spp.*)	48:1
Fir (*Abies spp.*)	77:1		

Bare-root (dormant) plants are shipped in late autumn and must be installed immediately — to all intents and purposes they are asleep or anaesthetized, and it's crucial that you don't wake them up by subjecting them to warm temperatures. These sorry-looking twigs and unpromising bits of root remain somnambulant for the duration of the winter, only to awaken in the spring, without even knowing that they've been moved. This same principle applies to most woodland trees, shrubs, and bulbous plants; the gardener is actually deceiving them into thinking they haven't been tampered with in the least.

Most of the ground-level or herbaceous plant material that is suitable for woodland gardens blooms during the spring, and the reason is simple: Across most of North America, deciduous woodland leaf canopies are generally fully expanded by early June, so if woodland flowers are to bloom, photosynthesize (in order to store energy for next year's flowers), and set seed, they must do so quickly.

This is part of the reason that many woodland flowers have permanent underground storage facilities in the form of tubers, bulbs, rhizomes, and corms. They provide an extra insurance policy against the coming year, enabling plants to survive drought, floods, and forest fires. It's a curious concept, but most of these springtime plants actually experience their seasonal autumn phase before the rest of us have even started to think about planting out the tomatoes.

Woodland gardeners must also bear in mind that if they choose to plant coniferous evergreens, these trees and shrubs will necessarily cast dense shade all year long, so they must be placed strategically (keeping them on the garden periphery often solves this dilemma). It's also important to be cognizant of the ultimate size of each tree before you purchase it, especially in relation to your house — North America already has a surplus of small bungalows flanked by two gigantic spruce trees, thank you very much. Also, be aware of the eventual size of each tree's canopy and its shape, and remember that in most cases, the root system will wander far beyond the drip line of the tree. Most nurseries that supply woody plant material will be happy to give you one of their catalogues, which will contain this sort of information, enabling you to peruse it at leisure.

In a mature woodland, conditions on the forest floor may be vastly different compared to more exposed areas nearby. In spite of the fact that the tree canopy will likely intercept over ten percent of the total rainfall, conditions at ground level are always more humid because of the protection from wind and evaporation that the larger trees provide. Temperatures are also moderated because of the canopy, remaining cooler in summer and warmer in winter.

This fact wasn't lost on Canadian pioneer plantswoman Catherine Parr Traill, who observed in 1885, "Although the snow lingers longer within the forest than on the opened, cleared lands to which the sun and wind have more ready access, yet vegetation makes more rapid advances, when once the Spring commences, within the shelter of the trees.

"No chilling, biting winds or searching frosts penetrate the woods,—to nip the early buds of leaf and flower as on exposed clearings. Within the forest all is quiet and warmth, when without, the air is cold and the wind blustering. It is among the bushes and low saplings that the first tints of early Spring verdure are seen; under the kindly nursing of the shrubbery we find the first Spring flowers and succulent plants."

Born in England in 1801, Traill emigrated to Canada in 1832, eventually finding herself (via birchbark canoe) in the virgin forests of what is now Lakefield (near Peterborough, Ontario). Over the next fifty years she wrote many books, most notably *The Backwoods of Canada,* followed by *The Canadian Settler's Guide* (1857), *Canadian Crusoes* (1859), *Canadian Wildflowers* (1868), and *Studies of Plant Life in Canada* (1885).

Woody plant material is best installed in late autumn when it is dormant. Pictured here is the doublefile viburnum (Viburnum plicatum subsp. tomentosum 'Mariesii'), a cultivar that has been around since the 1870s and that adds instant architectural interest to the woodland margin.

Many of our native woodland flowers bloom during the spring, before unfurling tree leaves block out all the sunlight. Indigenous species such as (l to r) spotted geranium (Geranium maculatum), Jack-in-the-pulpit (Arisaema triphyllum), woodland phlox (Phlox divaricata), and yellow lady's slipper (Cypripedium calceolus) are well adapted to these quirky woodland rhythms.

While the earlier volumes were primarily intended to encourage emigration from England to British North America, Mrs. Traill wasn't one to paint an unrealistically rosy picture, and her observations about "life in the backwoods" are nothing if not down to earth and practical. Later in her life, her interest focused more toward the indigenous flora of her new surroundings, and in spite of being rather preachy in tone, and definitely politically incorrect, these collections nevertheless reveal a keen natural eye and a genuine affection and admiration for the plant life of her adopted home. She writes lovingly of local lakes — Stony, Katchewanooka, and Rice — as well as her cherished Otonabee River, now part of the busy Trent Canal system. Of course, she wouldn't recognize it now, and I shudder to think what she'd have said about the zebra mussels!

As twenty-first-century gardeners busy themselves in worrying about diminishing natural habitats (as if we had invented the notion), and rush to restore natural woodlands (while muttering under our breath about ozone depletion and the need for "greenspace"), it might be instructive to review what Catherine Parr Traill had to say about clear-cutting and the destruction of forests. Writing in 1885 (at the age of eighty-four), and having dedicated her book *Studies of Plant Life in Canada* to the governor general (The Marquis of Lansdowne), she made an earnest appeal to the fledgling eighteen-year-old Canadian government:

"It seems now to be an established fact that the climate of many countries has been materially affected by the total destruction of its native forests. If this be so, then surely it behoves the legislators of this country to devise laws to protect future generations from similar evils, by preventing the entire destruction of native trees. There are large tracts of Crown Lands yet in the power of the Government, and reserves might be made or laws enacted by which the valuable products of the soil might be in some measure protected. Let our wise, far-seeing statesmen see to it."

So you see, King Solomon really was right when he said "there is no new thing under the sun." As for our current "far-sighted" legislators, I would point out that over 115 years later, *we're still waiting!* In any case, even if you can't be personally responsible for what was lost generations ago, you can certainly take charge of your own land and attempt to re-establish some of these forfeited treasures before they disappear forever.

Selecting which trees and shrubs you would like to include in your woodland garden is something that will take you some time to decide, and I would encourage you not to rush into anything, and to absolutely avoid impulse purchases. Trees and shrubs are long-term investments, and unlike herbaceous plants, it's difficult to move them once they're in place. Use the charts in the previous chapter to steer you in the right direction: Remember

to consider the pH level of your native soil, try to include tap-rooted woody material whenever possible, plant for longevity, and aim to plant trees and shrubs that will produce flowers (or fruit and nuts) as well as leaves.

While I have concentrated principally on our oft-overlooked native tree and shrub species, don't feel that this places a restriction on you when it comes to choosing plant material. I'm a sucker for French lilacs (*Syringa vulgaris* and cvs.) and wouldn't dream of advising you to eschew them simply because they aren't native to North America. What I would caution you about is the possibility of mildew problems, leaf blights, and a host of nasty insects that might invade your woodland margin. Problems like these are more severe in some parts of the continent than in others, so it pays to chat up your neighbours and local nursery staff if you're unsure about potential problems in your area. Look before you jump, but don't be put off simply because a plant didn't evolve on our shores!

Once your woodland garden is in place, you will have to keep a close eye on it for the first two or three years. Newly installed plants must be kept watered while they establish their permanent root systems. Compost and leaf mould should be added at least annually until your new plants are able to provide sufficient quantities for themselves.

By the end of the third year, you can give up woodland maintenance in favour of woodland management. Removing unwanted plants will likely become a seasonal chore, as will encouraging young plants to establish themselves in preparation for their eventual take-over from older specimens. Like all gardeners, the woodlander will need to inspect plants for disease and insect afflictions, but the idea is more to monitor than to interfere. Whatever you do, don't become too fastidious in your upkeep and maintenance. Healthy, well-balanced woodlands depend on natural succession, so if an old tree dies and falls down, leave it. Woodpeckers will snap up the millions of insects that will soon invade it, and it will provide shelter and cover for small mammals before eventually being reclaimed by the forest floor that nurtured it. And the beat goes on…

Catherine Parr Traill would no doubt be reassured to see the great white trillium (Trillium grandiflorum) still blooming resolutely each spring by the shores of her beloved Stony Lake.

NAME:
Canada columbine
(*Aquilegia canadensis*)
HEIGHT:
30 to 60 cm (1 to 2 feet)
HARDY TO:
Zone 3
EXPOSURE:
Part sun to full shade
BLOOMING PERIOD:
Mid-spring to midsummer
SOIL:
Tolerant of dry woodland soil
COMPANIONS:
Associates well with hardy geraniums, especially mourning widow (*Geranium phaeum*) and wood cranesbill (*G. sylvaticum* 'Mayflower') and with *Astilbe* cultivars
SPECIAL NOTES:
Canada columbine is far less troubled by leafminer than other species, but if it's a problem, cut plants back to ground level and discard infested leaves. Keep plants watered until new foliage appears (7 to 14 days).

canada columbine

aquilegia canadensis

Unlike its well-known and popular relation, European columbine (*Aquilegia vulgaris*), Canada columbine is not much grown in North America except in strictly native gardens, although it has contributed more than a few genes to many of our more familiar hybrid strains.

Native from Nova Scotia to the Northwest Territories, south to Nebraska, Texas, and Florida, its range stretches across the continent, verifying what an adaptable, carefree plant it really is, assisted in this to a great degree by its firm, stout taproot. Possessing a light, airy stature and ranging in height from 30 to 60 cm (1 to 2 feet), it bears nodding red and yellow flowers with stiff, upright spurs 1.5 cm (½ inch) long, and is hardy from Zones 3 to 8.

Seen to advantage growing on the woodland margin, Canada columbine will benefit from an hour or two of sun each day, although it will tolerate full shade conditions and seems perfectly content in dry soil. Pollinated by hummingbirds and those insects capable of furnishing a sufficiently long proboscis, Canada columbine will self-seed around your garden generously once it's established.

A member of the buttercup family (Ranunculaceae), the *Aquilegia* genus contains about seventy species, of which fifteen are native to North America. *Aquilegia canadensis* was the first of these species to be sent back to England, courtesy of the famous seventeenth-century plant collector, John Tradescant Jr., who was also responsible for introducing other native North American plants to Europe such as his namesake, *Tradescantia virginiana* (spiderwort) and *Rudbeckia laciniata* (yellow coneflower). In 1637 he sent plants (and seeds for insurance) of *Aquilegia canadensis* from Virginia to his father in London, John Tradescant Sr., who incidentally was gardener to King Charles I.

This charming plant has been grown in top-notch European gardens ever since, and I think it's high time we repatriated it! Blooming dependably from mid-spring to midsummer, it takes over nicely after the first flush of spring flowers have faded, and it will continue to bloom sporadically until autumn. The great British garden writer Margery Fish was enthusiastic about Canada columbine, and it still blooms at her former home, East Lambrook Manor (in Somerset), although she cautioned that "the gold and red of *Aquilegia canadensis* needs white flowers to tone down its brilliance. By accident I planted *Paradisea liliastrum* (St. Bruno's lily) nearby and its small delicate flowers near the aquilegia made light relief." Since St. Bruno's lily is hardy only to Zone 7, gardeners in colder zones can easily achieve the same effect by instead planting spring snowflake (*Leucojum vernum*) or summer snowflake (*L. aestivum*), both of which are hardy to Zone 4.

Gardeners west of the Rockies may prefer to grow *Aquilegia formosa*, the western representative of *A. canadensis*. Native from Alaska to California and hardy to Zone 4, it is almost identical to Canada columbine except that its flowers are slightly larger (2 cm / ¾ inch), and the colour of the outside petals (sepals, really) tend to be more orange than scarlet.

Columbines are a promiscuous lot, hybridizing freely with one another, so we shouldn't ignore some of the European varieties that deserve a little space in North American naturalized gardens. Principal among these is the European *Aquilegia vulgaris* (Granny's bonnet), and especially the cultivar 'Nora Barlow', which, when grown in isolation, will produce true-to-type seedlings. The alpine columbine (*Aquilegia alpina*) bears gorgeous blue flowers with 2.5 cm (1 inch) long spurs and is a spirited self-seeder that remains undeterred even by sea-level surroundings.

Most of the *Aquilegia* we see for sale in garden centres are complex hybrids of the Canadian *A. canadensis*, the Tex-Mex *A. longissima*, and the European *A. vulgaris* — a genial composition of nationalities embodied florally, I always like to think. The result of these various combinations can be seen in strains such as the 'Biedermeier Group', the 'McKana Hybrids', and the 'Mrs. Scott-Elliot Hybrids', all of which are hardy to Zone 3, and all of which will persist with their shameless botanical hanky-panky in your garden for generations to come. This is a good thing, because eventually you'll end up with your own strain of plants, especially suited to the conditions that prevail in your garden. It's all very Darwinian.

The first of our native Aquilegia *species to be introduced into European gardens (in 1637), Canada columbine is native from Nova Scotia to the Northwest Territories. Content to grow in the dry, semi-shaded conditions of the woodland margin, it battles for space in my garden with cowslips* (Primula veris) *and sweet violets* (Viola odorata).

NAME:
Deadnettle
(*Lamium maculatum*)
HEIGHT:
20 cm (8 inches)
HARDY TO:
Zone 3
EXPOSURE:
Part shade; the species
form is able to tolerate
denser shade than are
the cultivars
BLOOMING PERIOD:
Late spring to midsummer
SOIL:
Performs best in a soil rich
in humus and leaf mould
COMPANIONS:
Works well around the
base of woody plant mate-
rial and large ferns, or can
be left to battle it out with
other woodland ground-
covers such as lily-of-the-
valley (*Convallaria majalis*),
English ivy (*Hedera helix*), or
sweet violets (*Viola odorata*)
SPECIAL NOTES:
Keep plants well watered
during dry spells while they
are becoming established.

deadnettle

lamium maculatum

Deadnettle is a plant from Eurasia that performs the same sort of function in the garden that sweet woodruff does — providing a colourful mat of flowers and foliage on the floor of the woodland and woodland margin.

Preferring at least two hours of sunlight each day, deadnettle is best grown in partly shaded conditions rather than in the dense shade that sweet woodruff is able to tolerate. Growing to a height of about 20 cm (8 inches) and hardy to Zone 3, deadnettle has flowers that may be white, pink, or purple, and there is also quite a choice in leaf colour, from the standard mid-green splashed with white or pink, to silvery white, and even a golden yellow form.

Deadnettles flower from late spring to early summer and so associate well with some of the larger spring-flowering bulbs such as single late tulips (*Tulipa* cvs.), crown imperials (*Fritillaria spp.*), and snowflakes (*Leucojum spp.*). I also like to use dead-nettle around the base of larger shade-loving perennials that may be slow to emerge in the spring: hostas (*Hosta spp.* and cvs.), Japanese anemones (*Anemone × hybrida* cvs.), and yellow wax bells (*Kiringeshoma palmata*). Deadnettles are also superb when placed at the foot of deciduous trees and shrubs, particularly when the blossoming time of each coincides, as it often does, with azaleas and rhododendrons (*Rhododendron spp.* and cvs.).

The common name of deadnettle must have developed because the leaf of this species so closely resembles that of stinging nettle (*Urtica dioica*), but it can be distinguished from the latter by its square, hollow stems, and of course, the absence of stinging hairs. The botanical name is derived from the Greek *laimos*, meaning "throat," and alluding to the shape of the flowers that resemble diminutive snapdragons (*Antirrhinum spp.*), and, in fact come close to approximating an open throat.

Like most of the plants that perform well in woodland conditions, deadnettle spreads vegetatively by underground rhizomes (modified storage stems) and stolons (runners), and this arrangement works well, making the plant both drought tolerant and easy to propagate by division. If a patch of deadnettle becomes too overgrown, it's easy to pull out the shallow roots, but be prepared to endure an acrid, unpleasant odour (emanating from the disturbed rhizomes) while you do so.

Although rarely bothered by insect pests, the plants may begin to look ragged by midsummer during especially hot and dry years. If this is the case, cut back all foliage to

One of the showier woodland groundcovers, Lamium maculatum is vigorous without being
invasive. Perfect under deciduous trees and shrubs, most lamiums will appreciate a few hours
of sunlight per day early in the season. Be sure to experiment with the numerous cultivars
available commercially.

Although I find the pink-flowered species form of *Lamium maculatum* to be the most adaptable to the widest range of conditions, there are also many cultivars available for woodland gardeners to experiment with. Some of the most popular include the following:

Lamium f. album • Silver and green leaves, white flowers

'Angel Wings' • Dark green leaves with a central silver stripe, pink flowers

'Aureum' • Yellow leaves with a white blotch, pink flowers. Requires more sun and is less robust than other cultivars.

'Beacon Silver' • Silver leaves with a green edge, pink flowers. Leaf spot is sometimes troublesome.

'Beedham's White' • Chartreuse leaves, white flowers

'Chequers' • Green and silver leaves, deep pink-purple flowers. A vigorous grower

'Pink Pewter' • Green, silver, and grey leaves, pink flowers

'Shell Pink' • Green leaves with a central silver stripe, pink flowers. One of the longest-blooming cultivars

'White Nancy' • Foliage similar to 'Beacon Silver', but with pure white flowers. Excellent for brightening up a dark corner

Summer snowflake (Leucojum aestivum) represents one of the larger spring bulbs that work well in association with groundcovers like deadnettle (Lamium maculatum). Looking a little like lily-of-the-valley (Convallaria majalis) on steroids, summer snowflake is also a good substitute for the more tender St. Bruno's lily (Paradisea liliastrum).

ground level and irrigate thoroughly. Within ten to fourteen days, fresh growth will appear and will continue to look green and lush until the first snowfalls.

It would be remiss of me to leave the deadnettles without mentioning *Lamium galeobdolon* (syn. *Lamiastrum galeobdolon*) or yellow archangel. It's a plant I've never been quite sure about, with its dark foliage and yellow flowers — not to mention its invasive tendencies — in fact, it's always seemed slightly sinister to my way of thinking.

I'm also irritated by its constant botanical re-classification. Four hundred years ago it was considered a *Lamium*, but was subsequently assigned a genus of its own — not once, but twice! First as *Galeobdolon*, and then as *Lamiastrum*, which is what I first learned to call it. Now it's a *Lamium* again.

Taller (to 50 cm / 20 inches), and more aggressive than its *L. maculatum* relatives, it requires close monitoring, or it may overtake less aggressive woodland inhabitants. The cultivar 'Herman's Pride' is the selection most often seen in commerce and is somewhat better behaved than the species form; also available is 'Variegatum' and 'Compacta'. It's an acquired taste, and one of those plants that most people either love or hate. Approach with caution.

NAME:
Hardy geranium
(*Geranium spp.*)

HEIGHT:
Varies among *spp.*, 50 to
60 cm (20 to 24 inches)
on average

HARDY TO:
Zones 3 to 4

EXPOSURE:
Part to deep shade

SOIL:
Ordinary woodland soil.
Amend with compost
and leaf mould during
installation.

COMPANIONS:
Perfect around the base of
woody plant material. Also
associates well with bleeding heart (*Dicentra formosa*),
purple foxglove (*Digitalis
purpurea*), *Houttuynia cordata*
'Chameleon', and *Cardamine
pentaphyllos* (syn. *Dentaria
digitata*)

SPECIAL NOTES:
All *Geranium spp.* will
appreciate a haircut (down
to ground level) after flowering. In addition to a fresh
flush of foliage, a second
set of blooms are often
produced.

hardy geranium

geranium spp.

Not to be confused with the *Pelargonium spp.* that are commonly called geraniums, "real" geraniums are generally hardy to Zones 3 or 4, and are long-lived, carefree plants. A large genus containing over three hundred species, most require sunnier conditions than our naturalized woodland garden is able to provide, but there are certainly a few representatives that are tolerant of dry shade and should be included in every woodland scheme.

The first of these is the bigroot geranium (*Geranium macrorrhizum*), which is native to southern Europe. Introduced to Britain from Italy in 1596, it caught on quickly and is mentioned in a list of plants being grown at the Oxford Botanic Garden in 1658; since then, gardeners have never looked back!

Reaching a height of about 50 cm (20 inches), and bearing clusters of purple, pink, or white flowers, *Geranium macrorrhizum* provides the perfect solution for difficult woodland spots where little else will thrive. Steadily increasing to form a luxuriant, weed-proof mat, it would appear at first glance that the plant is spreading via underground roots, but in fact, it spreads in much the same way that strawberries (*Fragaria spp.*) do. The thick horizontal stems (or rhizomes) it sends out (which behave like runners) can often move more than 30 cm (1 foot) away from the mother plant before re-rooting at a growth node on the runner.

By purchasing only two or three plants, you will be able to cover a large area in just a few years. Plants may be installed at any time of the year (although spring or autumn planting is preferred) in average woodland soil that has been amended with some extra compost or leaf mould to get them off to a good start. Once the mother plants begin to spread, the fleshy rhizomes can be snapped off, leaving some fibrous roots on the bottom, and just three or four leaves on the top. Believe it or not, they're now ready for transplanting! Bury the detached rhizomes in 3 to 4 cm (1 to 1 ½ inches) of soil, water them in thoroughly, and within a few weeks, you'll have flourishing new clumps scattered around the base of trees and shrubs. Because their roots are so close to the surface, they

One of my favourite plants, Geranium phaeum *scoffs at dry shade. Although commonly called "mourning widow," I think that "merry widow" would constitute a better name, since the merest breeze will induce the widow to lift her skirts and dance a gleeful can-can above her platform of pale green leaves.*

In addition to the straight species form of *Geranium macrorrhizum*, there are several cultivars available which will enable to you enlarge your colour palette:

'Album' • Introduced from Bulgaria by plant collector and nurseryman Walter Ingwersen; white flowers

'Bevan's Variety' • Deep magenta flowers with red sepals

'Ingwersen's Variety' • One of the sturdiest forms with soft pink flowers. Widely available

'Lohfelden' • From Germany, pink flowers with dark pink veins

'Variegatum' • A good foliage plant bearing purplish-pink flowers. Requires more moisture and light than other cultivars

A perfect plant for dry, shady conditions, the almost black flowers of *Geranium phaeum* look especially dramatic when planted under trees and shrubs with golden foliage. Check your local nursery for any of the following cultivars:

'Album' • Large, clear white flowers with golden anthers. Contrasts well with dark-flowered cultivars

'Langthorn's Blue' • Violet-blue flowers

'Lily Lovell' • Light green foliage, deep mauve flowers

var. *lividum* • Pale lilac or lavender flowers, unmarked leaves. *G.* var. *lividum* has produced two further cultivars — 'Joan Baker' and 'Majus'

'Samobor' • Leaves are heavily blotched with chocolate brown markings, dark purple flowers. Very choice

'Variegata' • Leaves are margined with creamy yellow, and irregularly splashed with reddish pink streaks. Less vigorous than other cultivars

won't disturb neighbouring plants, and since their rhizomes store both nutrients and water, they are tough and drought-resistant customers.

The leaves of bigroot geranium have been described by some as aromatic, but I don't care at all for the bitter stench they leave on your hands after working with them for a while. The main flush of flowers occurs in early summer, with a few bonus flowers late in the season as autumn approaches. The foliage of most *Geranium spp.* and cultivars can sometimes begin to look tatty during the dog days of summer, and if this is the case, the remedy is simple. Cut all foliage back to ground level and irrigate well. New foliage will appear in a week or two, and this chopping back of plants seems to encourage sporadic autumn flowering.

The hardy geranium that is able to cope with the driest, densest shade also happens to be one of my all-time favourite plants, bar none: *Geranium phaeum* or mourning widow (height to 70 cm / 28 inches). Introduced to Britain from Europe at about the same time as *G. macrorrhizum,* the common name refers to its dark purple, almost black flowers. Its leaves echo the theme, each one divided into seven lobes, and each lobe bearing a dusky, dark blotch at its base. An elegant plant by anyone's standards.

Geranium phaeum experiences its first flush of flowers in late spring and can be treated in much the same way as *G. macrorrhizum,* responding even more quickly to a post-flowering mow-down. Mourning widow will form a large clump quickly, so that propagation by division is simple and speedy, and you will also be rewarded with plenty of new seedlings, often in the first year.

There are now several cultivars of *Geranium phaeum* available, but I was fortunate enough to be introduced to the best of these by the man who raised it, British *Geranium* authority, Trevor Bath. An improvement over the species, 'Lily Lovell' (named after Trevor's mother) has larger flowers (3 to 4 cm / 1 to 1 ½ inches across) of a deep, rich

Another excellent choice for dry shade, the woodland geranium (G. sylvaticum 'Mayflower') blooms in late spring, just as the bulbs are fading. Native to Eurasia and hardy to Zone 4, it bears rich, upward-facing violet-blue flowers (to 4 cm / 1 ½ inches across) which are held well above its deeply cut foliage.

mauve that are set off by its light green foliage. 'Lily Lovell' will accept dry shade with the same composure as the species form does.

I always feel slightly distressed that hardy geraniums seem to be so little-known in gardening circles, despite the efforts of the very best garden writers over the past 150 years. In *The Wild Garden* (1870), William Robinson campaigned relentlessly for more widespread inclusion of *Geranium spp.* in naturalized gardens. E. A. Bowles (1865–1954) continued to lavish praise on these plants in his classic discourse *My Garden in Summer* (1914), and subsequently indoctrinated Margery Fish, who in turn became known as a *Geranium* expert, inspiring a new generation of enthusiasts, including Trevor Bath. In Wales, A. T. Johnson (1873–1956) of *Geranium* 'Johnson's Blue' fame also wrote enthusiastically about *Geraniums* in two books, *A Garden in Wales* and *A Woodland Garden*. And now that I've been enlightened by Trevor Bath, it's your turn! How's that for a horticultural legacy?

More *Geranium spp.* that will tolerate dry shade:

G. × monacense (syn. G. *punctatum*) • With similar leaf markings to G. *phaeum* (one of its parents), and purplish-red flowers

G. nodosum • Bears funnel-shaped lilac-mauve flowers with dark purple veins from late spring to early autumn. Self-seeds nicely

G. × oxonianum 'Claridge Druce' • Named for Dr. G. Claridge Druce (1850–1932), onetime mayor of Oxford, this is a plant for difficult spots only. With roots that sink to China, it will grow and flower almost anywhere. Great for northern gardeners, but should be avoided in the Pacific Northwest, where it may become invasive

G. versicolor (syn. G. *striatum*) • Slightly off-white flowers with magenta veins and a romantic predilection for G. *endressii*. Never mind, their children are lovely

G. endressii • A refined plant that makes an excellent groundcover. Bright pink flowers with a silver sheen that become darker as they age. Hybrids between G. *versicolor* and G. *endressii* are now known as G. × *oxonianum*, and of these, 'Wargrave Pink' will accept the deepest shade

jacob's ladder

polemonium caeruleum

Containing only about twenty-five species, the *Polemonium* genus is an important, albeit small one, and though few in number it has given rise to sundry crosses, hybrids, and cultivars. In spite of the fact that many species are native to North America, they are so widely distributed in the wild that it would be equally legitimate to think of them as indigenous to much of Europe and Asia. In fact, Jacob's ladder is truly "a plant without borders," and recent research has shown that it was common in Britain and Europe as long ago as the Late Glacial period (c. 10,000 BCE).

Polemonium caeruleum is the species with which gardeners are most familiar, particularly since it recently gave rise to one of the hottest (and most expensive) cultivars to hit the sales floor in years: the variegated *P.c.* 'Brise d'Anjou'. But in spite of its instant status as a "brag plant," this new cultivar sprang from very humble roots, since the fragrant, bell-shaped blue flowers (1 to 2 cm / ½ to ¾ inch across) of Jacob's ladder have been enjoyed in unpretentious cottage gardens for centuries.

I grew my first plants from seed, which is as simple as sprouting beans, and much easier on the budget than buying nursery-grown stock. If seeds are started in early spring, plants should reach maturity and flower within the first year or two, so it's a good species for impatient propagators. Although individual plants aren't particularly long-lived (about five years on average), they are efficient self-seeders, so that once established in your woodland garden, their presence will definitely be felt over the long term.

Most British garden writers recommend that Jacob's ladder be grown in full to part sun, but this isn't good advice for North American gardeners. Not only are our summers much hotter than British ones, they are also considerably drier and sunnier, and because of this, plants in North America prefer the cooler conditions that partially to moderately shaded areas will provide. Planted at the base of shrubs and on the woodland margin, Jacob's ladder (hardy to Zone 3) will provide a multitude of grape bubblegum-scented blooms for many weeks in early summer. Like hardy geraniums, the foliage of Jacob's ladder may begin to look unkempt by midsummer and should be treated in the same fashion: Cut it back to soil level, and a fresh mound of leaves will appear in several weeks and will last well into autumn.

I think I was first attracted to these plants because of their common name, which alludes to the biblical story of Jacob's dream (Genesis Ch. 28). Each leaf is made up of between nineteen and twenty-seven leaflets arranged horizontally along the central midrib,

NAME:
Jacob's ladder
(*Polemonium caeruleum*)
HEIGHT:
40 to 90 cm (16 to 36 inches)
HARDY TO:
Zone 3
EXPOSURE:
Part sun to moderate shade
BLOOMING PERIOD:
Early summer
SOIL:
Woodland soil with plenty of humus and leaf mould
COMPANIONS:
Associates well with bloodroot (*Sanguinaria canadensis*), masterwort (*Astrantia major*), wood betony (*Stachys officinalis*), and hellebores (*Helleborus spp.*)
SPECIAL NOTES:
Jacob's ladder looks best when clumped in groups of at least five to seven plants, so it makes sense to grow it from seed initially, and then to allow mature plants to set fresh seed every year after flowering.

*A carefree plant, and hardy
to Zone 3, Jacob's ladder
(Polemonium caeruleum) is
easy and inexpensive to propagate
from seed. Once established in the
woodland garden, it will provide
beautiful blue, grape bubblegum-
scented blooms for years to
come. Gardeners in the Pacific
Northwest may have better luck
with Himalayan Jacob's ladder
(Polemonium himalayanum)
or the indigenous salmon Jacob's
ladder (P. carneum).*

looking very much like a mini botanical "ladder." This arrangement also gave rise to the even older common name of "Greek valerian" since the leaves also resemble those of the unrelated medicinal herb valerian (*Valeriana officinalis*).

Polemonium caeruleum is also available in a white flowered form, *P.c.* var. *lacteum* (syn. 'Album'), and a few of these scattered among the blue-flowered types make for a sparkling woodland display. The green leaves of *P.c.* 'Brise d'Anjou' are distinctively marked with a pale cream-coloured edge, and this contrast, coupled with the plant's arresting architectural form, can make for an eye-popping display that is impossible to miss.

Most gardeners imagine that the variegated 'Brise d'Anjou' represents a horticultural breakthrough, the result of late twentieth-century science and breeding techniques, but in fact it's been with us for centuries. Philip Miller certainly grew it, calling it "*Polemonium vulgare, foliis eleganter variegatis*" (Common *Polemonium* with elegant leaf variegation) in the 1754 edition of *The Gardener's Dictionary*. He even gave propagation instructions for variegated varieties: "The variegated Kinds are preserved by parting of their Roots; because Plants raised from Seeds would be subject to degenerate, and become plain. The best time to part them is about *Michaelmas* [September 29], that they may take good Root before the cold Weather prevents them." Dividing these variegated forms is still the best way to increase your stock, although some gardeners prefer to perform the task in spring rather than autumn.

In addition to *Polemonium caeruleum*, there are many more Jacob's ladder species for gardeners to choose from. The following types will all accept moderate woodland shade:

P. carneum • **Salmon Jacob's ladder** • Native to the Cascades, the best choice for gardeners in the Pacific Northwest. Pink blossoms that fade to purple. Zones 6 to 8, height to 35 cm (14 inches)

P. himalayanum • **Himalayan Jacob's ladder** • Sometimes considered to be a variety of *P. caeruleum*, I remember this plant from my childhood days in Srinagar, Kashmir. Hardy to Zone 5, the cvs. 'Album', Gracile', and 'Variegatum' are occasionally available

P. **'Lambrook Mauve'** • Raised by Margery Fish and still going strong. Lilac-lavender flowers from late spring to early summer. Hardy to Zone 4, height to 45 cm (18 inches)

P. reptans • **Creeping Jacob's ladder** • Excellent groundcover for shady areas, native to eastern North America. Zones 3 to 9, height to 35 cm (14 inches). Cultivars include 'Alba', 'Blue Pearl', and 'Konigsee'

E. A. Bowles also grew variegated Jacob's ladder, and commented that "I have never felt the disgust for variegated foliage evinced by so many good gardeners, and in many cases I warmly admire it. For instance … *Polemonium caeruleum* in [its] widely different lines of variegation [is] to my idea delightfully delicate in colour harmonies." I'm reminded yet again of King Solomon's dictum!

The constant botanical re-classification of the various *Polemonium spp.*, coupled with their love of interbreeding, makes for a complex mess when attempting to sort out the ancestry of various cultivars. Nevertheless, two important native North American *Polemonium* species (*P. reptans* and *P. humile*) seem to have combined with *P. caeruleum* to produce some superior specimens.

Interestingly, the first *Polemonium humile* (syn. *P. boreale*) plants to be grown in Europe were raised in 1826 from seed collected by Dr. John Richardson, who had accompanied Captain Franklin on his overland search for the Northwest Passage in the Canadian north. This has, in turn, given rise to a new race of plants classified as *Polemonium × richardsonii*, although ironically, they are more likely to be a cross between *P. caeruleum* and *P. reptans* — so you see how complicated it can all become.

purple fumewort

corydalis solida

The *Corydalis* genus is a large one, containing over three hundred species, which are widely distributed across the northern hemisphere. Several of these are suitable for culture in naturalized gardens, and foremost among them is *Corydalis solida*, native to Eurasia and hardy from Zones 5 to 8.

Like so many plants that are well adapted to a woodland environment, *C. solida* has a modified root system in the form of small, nut-like tubers that store energy and nutrients for the following year. Known as a spring ephemeral, the leaves of *C. solida* emerge early in the spring and are followed shortly thereafter by red-purple, mauve-pink, or pure white flowers. Once the flowers have faded and the seeds have set, the plant disappears like a veritable garden fugitive — until the following spring! *C. solida* is similar to rue anemone (*Anemonella thalictroides*) in that it likes a fairly sunny situation early in the season, followed by cooler, shadier conditions as the tubers approach dormancy, making it another good candidate for placement under deciduous trees.

Purple fumewort reaches a height of only about 25 to 30 cm (10 to 12 inches), and I adore the way it insinuates itself among the other spring-flowering plants, its rich, deep shades contrasting with and modifying the more vibrant spring colours of primroses (*Primula spp.*) and miniature daffodils (*Narcissus spp.*), while its delicate foliage complements emerging fern fronds. Once its job is complete, it vanishes swiftly and completely, leaving no trace of its presence above ground, although you can be sure it has spread another 10 or 15 cm (4 to 6 inches) in either direction below the soil surface. What a well-behaved plant it is, never outstaying its welcome, never crowding out other plants, and always multiplying slowly but surely.

As with any large genus, there is a fair bit of confusion associated with the species themselves, and they are constantly being reorganized. *Corydalis cava*, also a native of Europe, is often confused with *C. solida*, but it can be distinguished from the latter by its hollow tubers, shorter stature (between 10 and 20 cm / 4 and 8 inches), and duskier, duller flowers. Nevertheless, both *C. cava* and *C. solida* may be identified and sold in

A spring ephemeral par excellence, Corydalis solida is shown here to great advantage beneath the light, filtered canopy of hardy rhododendrons. Notice how both species benefit from a generous layer of pine needle mulch.

Purple fumewort (Corydalis solida) compliments small spring bulbs such as glory-of-the-snow (Chionodoxa forbesii) and striped squill (Puschkinia scilloides) admirably. By early summer this happy trio will have vanished altogether — but fortunately the tentative spikes of Hosta (foreground) will have taken over nicely by then.

nurseries variously as *C. ambigua, C. bulbosa,* and *C. halleri,* but don't fret, you'll doubtless enjoy the results of any plant you procure under these obsolete synonyms.

Corydalis solida can be established easily from seed, or by purchasing dormant tubers, although I think that most gardeners obtain it like I did — from a neighbour. Certainly this is how our old friend Margery Fish acquired her plants: "I have had the soft lavender *Corydalis solida* ever since I have had a garden, because it was growing in a cottage garden nearby and I was given some." Absolutely the best way to appropriate it, in my opinion!

William Robinson recommended it in 1883 as "a pretty little plant for borders, for naturalising in woods, and also for the spring garden." Of my favourite garden writers, only E. A. Bowles furnishes a probationary assessment: "I have never yet made up my mind as to whether I like *C. bulbosa* [i.e., *C. solida*] to spread about or no. On the one hand it is so early and does no harm, but on the other hand it is not very attractive and takes up a certain amount of space."

Corydalis species are part of the much larger poppy family (Papaveraceae), and our native North American types are essentially kissing cousins to our indigenous bleeding heart (*Dicentra*) species. This close connection made for a certain amount of botanical confusion when these plants were first being catalogued. *Dicentra canadensis* (squirrel corn), a bleeding heart through and through, was often classified as *Corydalis canadensis,* a potentially fatal mistake since the genuine squirrel corn was used as a herbal tonic for syphilis and menstrual complaints during the nineteenth century. (All *Corydalis spp.* contain potentially poisonous alkaloids.)

In spite of this botanical snafu, in 1885 Catherine Parr Traill managed to single out two native *Corydalis* species worthy of garden attention, namely *C. aurea* (golden fumitory) and the more widespread *C. sempervirens* (pale corydalis). *C. aurea* should not be confused with *C. lutea* (yellow corydalis), that rugged European that loves to colonize sterile stone walls and rocky spots. In spite of its European background, I can't imagine my garden without this good-natured interloper, happy to spread itself about where no other plant will prosper. Flowering from midsummer until the first frosts, *C. lutea* is frequently considered a common plant, but as the revered plantsman Graham Stuart Thomas, OBE, says, "*C. lutea* is often looked upon as 'common' — but when did that epithet have any control over beauty?"

NAME:
Rue anemone
(*Anemonella thalictroides*)
HEIGHT:
15 cm (6 inches)
HARDY TO:
Zone 3
EXPOSURE:
Prefers spring sun followed
by summer shade, and
accordingly performs best
under deciduous trees and
shrubs
BLOOMING PERIOD:
Spring to early summer
SOIL:
Ordinary woodland soil
with plenty of humus
COMPANIONS:
Associates well with related
wood anemones (*Anemone
nemorosa, A. quinquefolia*),
sweet woodruff (*Galium
odoratum*), and the barren-
worts (*Epimedium spp.*)
SPECIAL NOTES:
Rue anemone possesses no
petals — its flowering parts
are known as sepals. In
most plants, sepals are the
green, petal-like structures
that encase and protect the
flower's inner petals and
reproductive parts, known
collectively as the calyx.

rue anemone

anemonella thalictroides

Rue anemone is a plant that is not well known in Canada or the United States, and barely known at all in Europe, which is why I bring it to your attention now. Native from New Brunswick and Maine south to Georgia, west to Oklahoma and then north to Minnesota and Manitoba, it is obviously capable of withstanding a huge range of environmental variables and is hardy from Zones 3 to 8. Its delicate appearance belies its brawny disposition, so you have no excuse not to include it in your woodland scheme.

Rue anemone likes to grow in average woodland conditions: It does especially well under deciduous trees and shrubs and favours a loose, humusy soil with plenty of leaf mould. Growing about 15 cm (6 inches) tall, rue anemone blooms from spring until early summer, a period of at least six weeks, and an unusually long span for a perennial woodland plant.

The dainty foliage closely resembles that of meadow rue (*Thalictrum spp.*), a fact reflected in both its common and botanical names. The flowers (about 2 cm / ¾ inch across) are actually composed of between five and ten brilliant white sepals — not petals at all — a characteristic that *Anemonella* shares with its *Anemone* relations. Belonging to the buttercup family (Ranunculaceae), rue anemone is also unusual because it is the only species in its genus. Usually a genus will contain many species, all of which are capable of breeding together and producing offspring similar to themselves, but rue anemone is a lonely botanical orphan.

Fortunately, botanical orphans sometimes mutate spontaneously, and indeed, this has occurred with rue anemone. In addition to the pure white single form, there is a pink double form available called 'Oscar Schoaf', which is often sold under the names 'Flore Pleno', 'Schoaf's Double', or 'Schoaf's Pink', and is well worth keeping an eagle eye out for.

Like so many native woodland flowers, rue anemone has small, tuberous roots that store sugars and starches in anticipation of the following year's growth, making them

Usually in bloom for at least six weeks during the spring, rue anemone is native from New Brunswick to Manitoba. Where summers are especially hot and dry, rue anemone may go dormant, only to return bigger and better the following spring. It is pictured here (l to r) with barrenwort (Epimedium × rubrum), *the emerging leaves of Spanish bluebells* (Hyacinthoides hispanica), *and sweet woodruff* (Galium odoratum).

I like to combine rue anemone (Anemone thalictroides) with red barrenwort (Epimedium × rubrum) in my garden. Most of the epimediums that we grow today are the result of complex crosses, and one of the most charming of these (pictured here) has to be yellow barrenwort (Epimedium × versicolor 'Sulfureum').

extra-impervious to unfavourable weather conditions, occasional attacks from slugs, and drought. While these tiny tubers are apparently edible, a friend of mine recently pointed out that this would be comparable to eating larks' tongues on toast! Nevertheless, rue anemone's root structure makes it easy to transplant at almost any time of the year.

Generally, plants will take a year to establish, and then a further year or two to really clump up, but once they hit their stride, they will begin to self-seed — tentatively at

What woodland garden would be complete without ferns in addition to flowering plant material? The following suggestions are for undemanding, easy-care specimens. Entries marked with an asterisk (*) are particularly speedy colonizers.

COMMON NAME	BOTANICAL NAME	HARDINESS
Maidenhair fern	*Adiantum pedatum*	Zones 2 to 8
Lady fern	*Athyrium felix-femina*	Zones 4 to 8
Japanese painted fern	*Athyrium niponicum*	Zones 4 to 9
* Hay-scented fern	*Dennstaedtia punctiloba*	Zones 3 to 8
Golden male fern	*Dryopteris affinis*	Zones 4 to 8
Male fern	*Dryopteris filix-mas*	Zones 4 to 8
Marginal wood fern	*Dryopteris marginalis*	Zones 2 to 8
* Ostrich fern	*Matteuccia struthiopteris*	Zones 2 to 7
* Sensitive fern	*Onoclea sensibilis*	Zones 2 to 9
Cinnamon fern	*Osmunda cinnamomea*	Zones 2 to 9
Interrupted fern	*Osmunda claytoniana*	Zones 2 to 8
Royal fern	*Osmunda regalis*	Zones 4 to 9
Christmas fern	*Polystichum acrostichoides*	Zones 3 to 9
Western sword fern	*Polystichum munitum*	Zones 6 to 9
* New York fern	*Thelypteris noveboracensis*	Zones 4 to 8
Netted chain fern	*Woodwardia areolata*	Zones 3 to 9

first, but eventually quite prolifically. Plants may also be divided (this will be the only way to propagate the sterile, double pink form) in the early spring, just as they begin to emerge.

Like bloodroot (*Sanguinaria canadensis*), during summers with very low rainfall, the leaves may pack up and disappear altogether, but never mind, they will return faithfully the following spring. In my own garden, I like to combine rue anemone with other spring flowers such as early lungworts (*Pulmonaria spp.*), Canadian wild ginger (*Asarum canadense*), and Spanish bluebells (*Hyacinthoides hispanica*).

*The ostrich fern (*Matteuccia struthiopteris*) is native to both North America and Asia and is reliably hardy to Zone 2. This species can cover a large area quickly since it not only produces spores, but also spreads through vigorous underground rhizomes (runners).*

NAME:

Sweet woodruff
(*Galium odoratum*)

HEIGHT:

20 to 25 cm (8 to 10 inches)

HARDY TO:

Zone 4 or 5

EXPOSURE:

Part to full shade

BLOOMING PERIOD:

Late spring to early summer

SOIL:

Average woodland soil,
requires some additional
watering while becoming
established

COMPANIONS:

Perfect under taller spring
bulbs, and stunning under
trees that bloom at the
same time, e.g., service-
berries (*Amelanchier spp.*),
dogwoods (*Cornus spp.*),
and crabapples (*Malus spp.*)

SPECIAL NOTES:

One of the few plants that
will thrive in dense shade
and among shallowly
rooted trees and shrubs

sweet woodruff

galium odoratum

As any garden designer or landscape architect will tell you, sweet woodruff (*Galium odoratum* syn. *Asperula odorata*) is an absolutely indispensable plant for difficult areas and should never be left out of any conversation that includes the word "shade." Quite simply, sweet woodruff can perform miracles where most groundcovers fear to tread, and can do so with considerable panache.

The *Galium* genus is a large one (containing over four hundred species), but only a handful are of any interest to gardeners, with *G. odoratum* heading the list. Impervious to dense shade, sweet woodruff takes like a duck to water in woodland conditions. A low-growing plant (height 20 to 25 cm / 8 to 10 inches), the leaves are arranged in circular whorls, so that several leaves (between six and nine) all emerge together at the same juncture, lending an agreeable symmetry to even the smallest clump. As if this weren't enough, for weeks on end in early summer sweet woodruff is crowned with pristine chalk-white flowers, arranged in cymes (branched flower clusters) made up of tiny white stars.

Native to European woodlands, this plant has the right personality for a naturalized setting. Fortunately, sweet woodruff isn't difficult to propagate, so it isn't expensive at garden centres, and certainly buying it as a relatively small plant will save you money. Transplants can be installed in the spring or autumn, and just a few plants will spread (via underground roots and runners) to form attractive patches, often within a single season. Because these roots lie just under the soil surface, transplants must be kept reasonably well watered during the first year. On the other hand, once established, if plants begin to wander beyond their legitimate margins, they are easy to pull up. If things aren't progressing as quickly as you'd like, dividing established clumps in spring or autumn will increase your stock post-haste!

In other words, this is a vigorous plant, not an invasive one, and as Graham Stuart Thomas points out, "it will harm nothing over two feet in height, plant or shrub," so

One of the most valuable plants for shady areas, after flowering the whorled leaves of Galium odoratum will provide an attractive emerald carpet on the floor of a mature woodland for the rest of the season. Native to Europe, it has been used for centuries as a "strewing herb" or deodorizer — which may explain in part why Queen Elizabeth I presented sprigs of it "to individuals she wished to favour."

*Our native wild ginger (*Asarum canadense*) will thrive in the same deep shade that sweet woodruff (*Galium odoratum*) tolerates, although its primeval purple flowers are borne at ground level — all the more reason to plant some graceful bleeding hearts (*Dicentra spectabilis*) nearby!*

it's eminently suited for placement around woody plants, as well as some of the larger herbaceous species, particularly deep-rooted ones. Untroubled by pests, and remaining evergreen for most of the year, sweet woodruff will command increased attention with each passing season.

A herb by rights, sweet woodruff has long been cultivated in Europe and has been employed in surprisingly diverse ways over the centuries. Its old English name is *woderove* or *wodrove* — presumably for its habit of roving through the woods — I imagine that the *rove* eventually evolved to *ruff* due to the arrangement of the leaves on the stem, resembling an Elizabethan collar ruff. The first reference in English to *woderove* comes to us by way of a popular song of the late thirteenth century:

Daisies in this dales,
Notes sweet of nyhtegales;
Each fowl song singeth.
The threstelcock him threateth "oo";
Away is our wynter woo [woe]
When woderove springeth.

In the garden, sweet woodruff is almost without scent, but when the leaves are dried, they impart a lively fragrance of fresh-mown hay. Once dry, the leaves turn a dark brown, almost a black colour, but it's at this point that the chemical constituent coumarin kicks in, providing the strong, vanilla fragrance. This virtue wasn't lost on the Elizabethans, and they enthusiastically employed the dried leaves for everything from stuffing mattresses and pillows to hanging it in doorways and strewing it on floors as an air freshener. Georgian gentlemen placed dry leaves in the cases of their pocket watches so that the fragrance could be inhaled while simultaneously checking the time — perhaps an early form of aromatherapy!

Sweet woodruff has also been used extensively in herbal medicine, although it is no longer recommended for human consumption due to its anticoagulant properties. In spite of this, it's still an essential ingredient in *Maitrank* (Maybowl), the traditional punch consumed in Austria and Germany on May Day (May 1). Bunches of dried sweet woodruff are steeped in a deserving Moselle or Rhine wine, and then "kicked up a notch" with orange slices and sugar.

Our native species of *Galium* tend to be too invasive to be considered as garden subjects — even in a naturalized setting, but I must admit to cultivating another European form — not for ornament, but for interest. *Galium verum* (Our Lady's bedstraw) prefers more sun and drier soil than sweet woodruff, and it is considerably less attractive: a rather leggy plant with small yellow flowers.

As its name would suggest, it also contains plenty of coumarin and was used for bedding, but it was also an important ingredient in cheese making. Used as a vegetable substitute for rennet (made from the stomach linings of unweaned calves), it both curdled the milk and imparted a yellow colour to the cheese produced from the curd. It should be noted (with due humility), that the technique has now been lost, and even the scientifically oriented brains at Reading Agricultural College in the United Kingdom failed to produce more than a thin layer of junket when they combined *G. verum* with warm milk. As for me, I continue to experiment. I'll crack this nut yet!

While local names aren't very instructive from a botanical point of view, they frequently provide fascinating bits of socio-cultural information. Here are a few examples of what our forebears might have called these woodland jewels:

Kiss-me-quick (Dorset)

Ladies-in-the-Hay (Wiltshire)

Musc de bois (Wood musk) (France)

New-mown hay (Nottinghamshire)

Star grass (Northumbria)

Sweethearts (Somerset)

Waldmeister (Master of the woods) (Germany)

Woodrep (Scotland)

NAME:
Trillium
(*Trillium spp.*)
HEIGHT:
Varies between species,
30 to 40 cm (12 to 16 inches)
on average
HARDY TO:
Zone 3 or 4 (most)
EXPOSURE:
Part to full shade
BLOOMING PERIOD:
Early to late spring
SOIL:
Good woodland soil rich
in leaf mould and humus
COMPANIONS:
Unlike some woodland
plants, most *Trillium*
perform well under both
deciduous and coniferous
trees and shrubs. *Trillium*
also associate well with
Virginia bluebells (*Mertensia
pulmonarioides*), May apple
(*Podophyllum peltatum*), and
wood poppies (*Stylophorum
diphyllum*)
SPECIAL NOTES:
Trilliums prefer autumn
installation and once
planted, they resent
disturbance.

trillium

trillium spp.

William Robinson felt that our native *Trillium grandiflorum* was "one of the most beautiful hardy plants," and I doubt that many North American gardeners would argue with him. Soon after my family came to Canada we bought a summer cottage in the Muskoka Lakes district north of Toronto, and I have vivid childhood memories of banks of white trilliums blooming under the bare branches of the mixed beech, birch, and maple forest. Small wonder then that the Ontario government chose it as its provincial flower.

The *Trillium* genus is not a particularly widespread one. There are about six species native to Eastern Asia (and to Japan in particular), a further seven native to western North America, with the remaining thirty-five or so hailing from eastern North America. Interestingly, there isn't any crossover between species as is so often the case with much of the plant kingdom. In other words, species from Japan are absolutely distinct from those found in the Pacific Northwest, which in turn are completely different to eastern North American species — situations very different from the ones we found when examining more gregarious genera like Jacob's ladder and columbines!

Most trilliums are quite adaptable in their soil and habitat requirements and will grow readily in most woodland gardens. The majority of species prefer a nearly neutral soil pH level (between 6.5 and 7.0) and require plenty of leaf mould and humus within the soil profile. Like most of the woodland plants we have been discussing, *Trillium spp.* develop thick rhizomes, and these "bulbs" are best purchased (and promptly planted) in mid to late autumn, when they are dormant. Plants are also frequently offered for sale "in the green" during the spring rush, but purchased this way, they often take a year or two to settle down.

There is of course a great debate waging about the number of *Trillium spp.* offered for sale that are, in fact, culled from the wild. After crusading for the cause myself, I eventually realized that I would never know for absolute certain the origin of the plants I purchased. Retailers are supplied by wholesalers, who are often supplied by God Knows Whom. Certainly you can ask whether the plants you are buying are greenhouse propagated, but chances are that the person you question won't really know for sure either. One guide is price: If the plants you purchase are outrageously expensive, there's a good possibility they spent several years in a greenhouse (costs have to be recouped). On the other hand, if they're inexpensive, and look as if they have "real" soil (rather than potting mixture) around their roots… well, you get the picture.

Trillium cuneatum is another species of Trillium *that is widely distributed in the wild. Due to its tendency to form clumps around the base of trees, coupled with an ironclad constitution, it is an ideal candidate for naturalized woodland gardens. Native to Kentucky and Tennessee, it is known locally as whippoor-will flower, purple toadshade, bloody butcher, and sweet Betsy!*

While there's no doubt that certain *Trillium spp.* are endangered in the wild, this can't be reasonably said about species like *T. cernuum* (nodding trillium), *T. erectum* (red trillium), or *T. grandiflorum* (white trillium), all of which enjoy a very widespread distribution and are extremely adaptable plants to begin with. I was brought up to believe that picking a trillium flower would kill the entire plant, but as I discovered much later in life, this is sheer nonsense.

I suspect that the inspiration for this stricture sprang from the fact that in order to pick flowers, one must also pick the leaves, thereby inhibiting photosynthesis and food production for the rest of the season. However, plants didn't develop rhizomes and other similar food storage units for nothing, and while it's true that plants that have had their leaves removed may not bloom the following year, they certainly don't snuff it either. In any case, I'm almost sorry to reveal the scam, since it certainly taught youngsters to respect nature, and to leave natural areas looking the same way they did when they were first discovered.

There are many *Trillium spp.* to choose from, but the following list will get you off to a good start:

Nodding trillium (*T. cernuum*) • Not particularly showy, since its white flowers hide beneath its leaves, but I admire its demure disposition. Native from Newfoundland west to Manitoba, Zones 3 to 7

Red trillium (*T. erectum*) • One of the first trilliums to flower; outstanding in the woodland garden. Easy to propagate and much used in hybridization. Native from the Maritimes and Gaspé Peninsula west to the Great Lakes, Zones 4 to 8

White trillium (*T. grandiflorum*) • Native to New Brunswick, Quebec, and Ontario, and the easiest species for the uninitiated. Also available in pink or double white forms, Zones 4 to 8

Western white trillium (*T. ovatum*) • The most widespread and floriferous of the western varieties, similar to *T. grandiflorum,* but blooms slightly earlier. Native from Vancouver Island and southern British Columbia to southwestern Alberta. Hardy to Zone 5 or 6

Painted trillium (*T. undulatum*) • One of the few species that requires an acid soil. Native from North Bay, Ontario, east to Nova Scotia; petals are white with red markings. Associated more closely with coniferous (than deciduous) forests, Zones 3 to 7

Toad trillium (*T. sessile*) • An early-flowering species with red-maroon flowers, and an iron-clad constitution. Prefers alkaline soils, native to the Great Lakes region and the American Midwest, Zones 4 to 8

The great white trillium (Trillium grandiflorum) is always seen to best advantage when combined with other native plants that bloom at the same time, such as woodland daffodil (Uvularia grandiflora) and Virginia bluebells (Mertensia pulmonarioides).

There's little doubt that Catherine Parr Traill didn't place any prohibition on the occasional springtime vase of trillium: "Nature has scattered with no niggardly hand, these remarkable flowers, over hill and dale, wide shrubby plain and shady forest glen. In deep ravines, on rocky islets, the bright snow white blossoms of the Trilliums greet the eye and court the hand to pluck them."

Coupled with the same mythology about picking trilliums was the idea that they take seven years to bloom from seed, and this notion was less far-fetched. In the past, various authors have suggested that periods of between ten and twenty years elapse before plants bloom from seed, but recent research has shown that in natural woodland areas, most species flower within five to seven years. Once installed, trilliums should be left alone except for an annual autumnal side dressing of compost and leaf mould.

the meadow
garden

The most practical approach for many home gardeners will be to use native prairie plants in a meadow setting. Flowering plants represent a fundamental component for attracting wildlife to your garden: Each blossom provides pollen and nectar for insects and butterflies, and in the autumn, their ripe seed heads are the principal source of food for songbirds.

The resurrection and restoration of natural prairie ecosystems has become a hot topic in recent years, and it certainly represents a worthy cause, but large-scale restoration is not an option for most home gardeners, particularly those living in urban areas. Restoring a genuinely authentic prairie garden takes a great deal of time and hard work, not only during preparation and installation, but forever after. Planting areas must be absolutely weed free (and kept that way), while periodic burning is required to achieve the best results, making it even less likely that homeowners will want to espouse this style in its purest form.

On the other hand, a meadow is technically a clearing in the woodland and represents the first stage of forest reclamation, perhaps the result of a forest fire, or of several trees that occupy the same space simply dying of old age. In nature, meadows eventually mature into woodlands, in anticipation of the cycle beginning all over again.

The approach to a meadow-style garden that I recommend is a hybrid between the prairie and the meadow. By using plants native to the prairies, we can recreate the appearance of a prairie in a meadow setting. In other words, rather than attempting to create a genuine prairie with all its maintenance and monitoring requirements, we instead create a sunny meadow containing plants that are found growing naturally in prairie areas. This approach makes it possible for gardeners from coast to coast to get a prairie feel without fear of incinerating their homesteads.

Prairie plants are less particular about soil than their woodland counterparts. Most average garden soil is suitable, but as with any garden, it should be improved with compost, shredded leaves and/or composted manure before new plants are installed. Meadow gardens also require plenty of sunshine and should not be attempted in areas that receive less than six hours of direct sunlight per day.

Irrigation is rarely an issue since most prairie plants are extremely drought tolerant. When you are establishing a new meadow garden, it's easier to buy transplants than to attempt starting everything from seed yourself. By purchasing one- to two-year-old plants, you'll be able to gauge more quickly and accurately which species will thrive in your landscape and which ones won't. As a general guideline, autumn-blooming plants are best installed in spring, while spring-blooming plants seem to do better when they're installed in the autumn.

When you're planning a naturalized meadow, bear in mind a few considerations. As with a woodland garden, meadow gardens should never look too manicured. Flowering plants will provide pollen for bees, nectar for butterflies, and eventually seed for songbirds. Leftover seed will increase your stock of plant material, so once again, avoid the temptation to deadhead 'til you drop! Unlike the woodland garden, whose principal flowering period

Heavy clay soils can present a formidable obstacle to many gardeners, but fortunately there are several native species that don't resent clay. Instead, their strong roots penetrate deeply through the soil profile, actually helping to loosen and aerate compacted sections:

Atlantic coreopsis (*Coreopsis tripteris*)	Zones 4 to 8	Ironweed (*Vernonia noveboracensis*)	Zones 4 to 9
Beebalm (*Monarda spp.*)	Zones 3 to 9	New England aster (*Aster novae-angliae*)	Zones 3 to 8
Black-eyed Susan (*Rudbeckia hirta*)	Zones 3 to 7	Purple coneflower (*Echinacea purpurea*)	Zones 2 to 9
Blazingstar (*Liatris spp.*)	Zones 3 to 9	Rattlesnake master (*Eryngium yuccafolium*)	Zones 4 to 8
Compass plant (*Silphium laciniatum*)	Zones 4 to 9	Showy sunflower (*Helianthus × laetiflorus*)	Zones 5 to 9
Cup plant (*Silphium perfoliatum*)	Zones 4 to 9	Smooth penstemon (*Penstemon digitalis*)	Zones 2 to 8
False indigo (*Baptisia australis*)	Zones 3 to 9	Yellow coneflower (*Ratibida pinnata*)	Zones 3 to 10

A consummate clay-buster, our native blazingstar (Liatris spicata) is easy to grow from seed. Unlike most plants that produce flowering spikes (e.g., delphiniums and lupins), the individual blossoms of blazingstar open from the top of the spike downwards, rather than from the bottom up.

> While we tend to think of prairie plants as hitting their stride from midsummer to autumn, don't overlook several spring-blooming species:
>
> | | |
> |---|---|
> | Canada columbine (*Aquilegia canadensis*) | Zones 3 to 8 |
> | Creeping Jacob's ladder (*Polemonium reptans*) | Zones 4 to 8 |
> | Pasque flower (*Pulsatilla patens*) | Zones 4 to 7 |
> | Prairie smoke (*Geum triflorum*) | Zones 1 to 5 |
> | Shootingstar (*Dodecatheon meadia*) | Zones 4 to 8 |
> | Spiderwort (*Tradescantia ohiensis*) | Zones 4 to 9 |
> | Spotted geranium (*Geranium maculatum*) | Zones 3 to 8 |
> | Wild lupine (*Lupinus perennis*) | Zones 3 to 9 |

All the silphiums are native to North America, and most are capable of reaching heights of 2.5 to 3 m (8 to 10 feet) at maturity. The compass plant (Silphium laciniatum) is especially idiosyncratic, since the flat sides of its leaves tend to point directly east or west, while its sunflower-like blooms generally face east, hence its common name.

occurs in spring, prairie plants bloom from spring to autumn, so you can plan to have something in bloom for most of the growing season. Finally, remember that plants grow naturally in clumps, so strive for drifts of colour, rather than for floral polka-dots.

Although most gardeners think of natural meadows as being devoid of woody plant material, this isn't always the case in natural settings. Towering oaks might look out of place in a meadow garden, but shrubs can play a vital role, particularly when it comes to providing shelter and food for wildlife.

In urban settings, a few judiciously placed shrubs will mean the difference between absolute exposure to the neighbours and some semblance of privacy. A shrub border skirting a prairie garden amounts to no more or less than curtains on a window (horticulturally speaking), and depending on the sort of parties you like to throw, both sorts of screening might prove appropriate.

Since we're creating a naturalized meadow rather than an authentic prairie grassland, you should also feel at liberty to include some suitable non-native species. I can't imagine my own meadow without bright spires of elecampane (*Inula helenium*), colourful drifts of yarrow (*Achillea* hybrids), or some of the less invasive buttercups (*Ranunculus spp.*); I would also be sorry to part with the hundreds of different daffodils (*Narcissus spp.* and cvs.*) I have interspersed throughout, and if you're lucky enough to find the bulbs, the Lady tulip (*Tulipa clusiana*) looks marvellous in a natural meadow setting.

I trust that when I grow up, I'll promptly develop a passion for grasses, but at the moment, I must admit I keep them to a minimum in my own landscape. Having said that,

Most prairies are composed of at least fifty percent grass, forty-five percent herbaceous (flowering) plants, and only five percent woody plant material. In contrast, meadows contain fewer grasses and are instead dominated by herbaceous plants, although the percentage of woody plant material remains constant at 5 percent. The following native shrubs will all look at home in a naturalized meadow setting while at the same time affording a sense of privacy:

NAME	MATURE HEIGHT	HARDY TO ZONE
Adam's-needle yucca (*Yucca filamentosa*)	1 m (3 feet)	5
Agriculture Canada Explorer roses (*Rosa* 'Explorer Series')	variable	3
Agriculture Canada Parkland roses (*Rosa* 'Parkland Series')	variable	2
Bayberry (*Myrica pennsylvanica*)	3 m (10 feet)	2
Black chokeberry (*Aronia melanocarpa*)	1 to 2 m (3 to 7 feet)	3
Bush cinquefoil (*Potentilla fruticosa*)	1 m (3 feet)	2
Carolina rose (*Rosa carolina*)	1 to 1.5 m (3 to 5 feet)	4
Clove currant (*Ribes odoratum*)	2 to 4 m (7 to 13 feet)	3
Common buttonbush (*Cephalanthus occidentalis*)	2 to 5 m (7 to 16 feet)	4
Common juniper (*Juniperus communis*)	1 to 2 m (3 to 7 feet)	2
Creeping juniper (*Juniperus horizontalis*)	0.5 m (20 inches)	2
Fragrant sumac (*Rhus aromatica*)	2 to 4 m (7 to 13 feet)	4
Hardhack spirea (*Spiraea tomentosa*)	1 to 2 m (3 to 7 feet)	4
Inkberry (*Ilex glabra*)	2 to 3.5 m (7 to 12 feet)	4
Inland ceanothus (*Ceanothus ovatus*)	0.5 to 1 m (20 to 36 inches)	3
Jerseytea ceanothus (*Ceanothus americanus*)	1 m (36 inches)	3
Leadplant amorpha (*Amorpha canescens*)	1 to 2 m (3 to 7 feet)	3
Prairie rose (*Rosa setigera*)	2 to 4 m (7 to 13 feet)	4
Prairie willow (*Salix humilis*)	2 to 4 m (7 to 13 feet)	3
Silver buffaloberry (*Shepherdia argentia*)	2 to 4 m (7 to 13 feet)	2
Silverberry (*Eleagnus commutata*)	2 to 4 m (7 to 13 feet)	2
Western snowberry (*Symphoricarpos occidentalis*)	1 to 2 m (3 to 7 feet)	2

they are an important component of any meadow area and help to frame and support the blooms of the flashier herbaceous plants. Grasses are easy to plant in-between and beside flowering meadow plants without fear of root competition. The shallow grass roots won't interfere with the much deeper roots of herbaceous plants, making them natural companions.

While most gardeners will want to concentrate their efforts on installing native grass species, don't be afraid to open up your borders to some of the more well-behaved globetrotters. For instance, I'd hate to be without my bold Asian zebra grass (*Miscanthus sinensis* 'Zebrinus'), its horizontally striped leaves easily commanding as much attention as any flower.

The following native grasses will all adapt to a wide variety of soil and climate conditions. Long-lived and drought tolerant, their autumn seed heads are both graceful and an important food source for wildlife, particularly during the winter months.

NAME	HARDINESS
Big bluestem (*Andropogon gerardii*)	Zones 3 to 8
Indian grass (*Sorghastrum nutans*)	Zones 3 to 8
June grass (*Koeleria macrantha*)	Zones 1 to 8
Little bluestem (*Schizachyrium scoparium*)	Zones 2 to 8
Prairie dropseed (*Sporobolus heterolepsis*)	Zones 3 to 7
Sideoats grama (*Bouteloua curtipendula*)	Zones 3 to 8
Switch grass (*Panicum virgatum*)	Zones 4 to 8

These native grasses will tolerate partial shade, and are the best choices for planting under shrubs or beside tall perennials:

Blue wild rye (*Elymus glaucus*)	Zones 3 to 9
Bottlebrush grass (*Hystrix patula*)	Zones 3 to 8

*Since I couldn't possibly deny a strong predilection for daffodils (*Narcissus* spp. and cvs.) in general, I may as well confess to an unnatural passion for the poet's Narcissus (*Narcissus poeticus* var. recurvus) in particular. Simply put, no meadow garden should be considered complete without it!*

Although grasses and shrubs are an integral part of any meadow garden, it is the flowering plant material that will inevitably provide the visual sizzle. The following seven plant suggestions will get you off to a good start, but this is a list that should be augmented yearly, not just to increase the diversity within your meadow, but also to deliver you from gardening complacency!

NAME:
Blue false indigo
(*Baptisia australis*)
HEIGHT:
To 1.5 m (5 feet)
HARDY TO:
Zone 3
EXPOSURE:
Best in full sun
BLOOMING PERIOD:
Late spring to early summer
SOIL:
Average to lean garden soil,
preferably on the dry side
COMPANIONS:
Blooms at the same time
as introduced herbaceous
species such as iris (*Iris
spp.* and cvs.) and peonies
(*Paeonia spp.* and cvs.).
I grow mine against a
backdrop of *Clematis* cvs.
('Hagley Hybrid', 'Henryi',
'Mrs. Cholmondeley',
'Vyvyan Pennell') and the
antique painted damask
rose 'Leda'.
SPECIAL NOTES:
Once it's installed, leave
blue false indigo alone.
Plants resent disturbance,
and frequent division of
plants should be avoided.

blue false indigo

baptisia australis

I fell in love with blue false indigo the very first time I saw it blooming in a friend's garden, and my ardour has remained constant ever since. Of the twenty or so species of *Baptisia,* all are native to North America, but as is the case with most genera, only a small number are worthy of garden culture. The best of the bunch (and the hardiest, from Zones 3 to 9) is *Baptisia australis.* Due to the specific epithet *australis,* blue false indigo is often mistaken for a plant from Down-under, but the species name simply means "southern," so you can forego greeting your plants with a cheery "G'day," and keep the tin of Foster's for yourself.

The name *Baptisia* is derived from the Greek *bapto,* meaning "to dye," since the related species *B. tinctoria* (wild indigo) was used in colonial days as a cheap substitute for true indigo (*Indigofera tinctoria*), which has been used to dye textiles a rich blue colour for millennia. Interestingly, *Baptisia tinctoria* was used by Native Americans to treat snakebite, and the Mohican tribe distilled the roots to bathe cuts and wounds, a practice that was adopted by the early settlers. Recent studies in Germany have indicated that root extracts may be useful in stimulating the immune system, but the jury is still out since it has also been shown that large or frequent doses may be harmful to humans. So if I were you, I'd leave the roots in the ground where they belong for the time being.

Baptisia australis is a substantial plant, and although slow to establish, it is extremely long-lived and will ultimately form a large clump, up to 70 cm (28 inches) across. The pale, sea-green leaves are crowned in late spring and early summer with luscious, deep blue flowers held aloft on multi-flowered racemes. Individual blooms resemble those of other members of the Fabaceae (or Legume) family, such as sweet peas and lupines, and *Baptisia* species also share the family talent for fixing atmospheric nitrogen through specialized nodes in their roots, actually improving the soil as they grow.

Blue false indigo is a carefree plant, requiring little or no maintenance. After flowering, plants may be deadheaded, although many flower arrangers covet their dark brown

Our native North American blue false indigo (Baptisia australis) is one of the naturalized meadows' longest-lived plants. Capable of fixing atmospheric nitrogen through specialized root nodes, it actually improves the soil as it grows. After it flowers, I allow a few seed pods to develop for rapacious black-capped chickadees.

seed pods (as do neighbourhood chickadees). Unfortunately, *Baptisia australis* is not an efficient self-seeder, but plants may be divided every four or five years to increase stock. It's a plant that's drought tolerant in the extreme, and its deep, woody roots may require some attention from your machete when the time comes to separate them. Happy in average garden soil (very rich soils may reduce bloom), blue indigo needs to be placed where you want it and then to be left alone. All *Baptisia spp.* resent disturbance, and instead seem to thrive on neglect.

Requiring a full sun location, after flowering blue false indigo assumes the size and stance of a small, handsome shrub (height to 1.5 m / 5 feet), and it will continue in this capacity until the first hard frosts, making it useful as a temporary summer screen or barrier.

In addition to the blue-flowered *Baptisia australis,* there are also some white-flowered forms that are almost as ornamental, and certainly equally insouciant. As with so many North American genera, *Baptisia* is a bit of a mess botanically, so these white-flowered forms may be sold under several different names, although the differences between them are (in my opinion) negligible. Suffice to say that plants sold under the names *Baptisia alba, B. lactea, B. leucantha,* or *B. pendula* are all lovely and will all associate well with the blue form, although they may be slightly less hardy (from Zones 4 to 8).

Not a species recommended for those gardeners devoted to instant gratification, blue false indigo is instead a plant more suited to the long haul and may actually outlive your grandmother's stand of heirloom peonies. And once you have it in your garden, you'll never want to be without it.

bottle gentian

gentiana andrewsii

Amidst the overwhelmingly golden hues of early autumn, floral respite may be found in the company of the last true blue bloomer of the year — bottle gentian. The *Gentiana* genus contains over four hundred species, many of which sport the same delectable cobalt-blue blossoms, so it isn't easy to stand out among such a talented bunch. Nevertheless, our native bottle gentian can hold its head high even amongst its flashiest relatives, while at the same time boasting one of the most peculiar floral shapes to be found in the meadow garden.

Native from Vermont and Quebec as far west as Saskatchewan and hardy to Zone 3, the tubular buds of bottle gentian never actually open, so that the 4 cm (1 ½ inches) long flowers look very much like azure dirigibles lined up for take-off along sturdy 45 cm (18 inches) high stems. It is due to this somewhat eccentric characteristic that Graham Stuart Thomas felt that *Gentiana andrewsii* was still a relatively unknown plant in most of Europe, despite its introduction in 1776: "Probably because its tubular flowers remain closed, this plant has never been widely grown." Even the infectiously enthusiastic plant collector Reginald Farrer (1880–1920) acknowledged that "*G. andrewsii* is the Gentian that never wakes up."

Certainly, it's true that gardeners like Thomas and Farrer were spoiled for choice when it came to gentians. Primarily native to alpine regions, most European species thrive in the cooler, moister conditions that prevail in northern Europe and our own Pacific Northwest. Unfortunately many of these alpine gentians are only hardy to Zones 6 or 7, and so do not fulfil the needs of gardeners living in colder zones.

Enter *Gentiana andrewsii*. Like Queen of the prairie (*Filipendula rubra*), many texts recommend that bottle gentian should be grown in moist, partly shaded conditions. Now does that sound like Saskatchewan to you? No. Instead we're clearly talking about a plant that affably contends and copes with an enormous number of climatic conditions, soil types, and moisture levels.

I grow my bottle gentians in an open sunny border that receives little or no supplementary water, and if it weren't for the fact that they are surrounded by taller perennials, the site would best be described as full sun, although in my garden it falls just short of that. Cultivated in this sort of situation, clumps of bottle gentian will increase steadily, if not swiftly.

Meriting a spot where it can be appreciated at close quarters, *Gentiana andrewsii* will relish a little pre-plant soil amendment in the form of compost, leaf mould, or

NAME:
Bottle gentian
(*Gentiana andrewsii*)
HEIGHT:
30 to 60 cm (1 to 2 feet)
HARDY TO:
Zone 3
EXPOSURE:
Full sun to part shade
BLOOMING PERIOD:
Late summer to late autumn
SOIL:
Average to rich garden soil
COMPANIONS:
Perfect with some of the smaller turtleheads (*Chelone spp.*), toad lilies (*Tricyrtis spp.* and cvs.) and variegated sedges (*Carex spp.*)
SPECIAL NOTES:
Although they are not widely available at nurseries, keep an eye out for some of our other native gentians, particularly the hardier (to Zone 4) closed gentian (*G. clausa*), and the recently re-classified fringed gentian, *Gentianopsis crinita* (syn. *Gentiana crinita*).

Native from Quebec to Saskatchewan and hardy to Zone 3, bottle gentian (Gentiana andrewsii) is possessed of one of the most bizarre floral silhouettes in the naturalized meadow — it's truly "the gentian that never wakes up."

well-composted manure, perhaps with a dash of bone meal thrown in for good measure. Once they're installed, leave the transplants alone as they resent upheaval, although I've had good success dividing three-year-old clumps in early spring — the trick here is to replant the divisions immediately. Left to their own devices, bottle gentians will self-seed, but never extravagantly, and seedlings will take a minimum of three undisturbed years before they proffer a blossom. They are slow but steady plants and are rarely bothered by disease or insect pests.

Many gentian species (particularly *Gentiana lutea*) have been singled out as useful in herbal medicine over the millennia, the first documented accounts having been discovered on a papyrus unearthed in an Egyptian tomb at Thebes (c. 1,200 BCE).

Nevertheless, the genus itself was named for Gentius, king of Illyria (now part of Albania), in the second century BCE, and was mentioned three hundred years later by the Roman physician Pliny and his Greek contemporary Dioscorides. Recommended since classical times as a digestive stimulant, *Gentiana lutea* is still an essential ingredient in Angostura bitters. The closely related *Gentiana macrophylla* (or *Qin jiao*) is one of the 252 herbs listed in the *Divine Husbandman's Classic* (*Shen'nong Bencaojing*), a Chinese herball written in the first century AD.

Closer to our own time, and on our own shores, Catherine Parr Traill attributed a different set of virtues to *Gentiana andrewsii*: "Our Gentians are the last tribute with which Nature decks the earth — her last brightest treasures — ere she drops her mantle of spotless snow upon its surface." She goes on to say, "We find our latest flowering Gentian in early September, and as late as November, if the season be still an open one, it may be seen among the red leaves of the Huckleberry (*Gaylussacia baccata*) and Dwarf Willows (*Salix spp.*), on our dry plains, above Rice Lake, and farther Northward. The Gentians seem to affect the soil on rocky islands and gravelly, open, prairie-like lands, among wild grasses."

William C. Bryant (1794–1878) certainly demonstrated a keen understanding and affection for autumn gentians when he wrote:

Thou blossom bright with Autumn dew,
And coloured with heaven's own blue,
That openest when the quiet light
Succeeds the keen and frosty night.

Thou comest not when Violets lean
O'er wandering brooks and springs unseen;
Thou waitest late, and comest alone
When woods are bare and birds are flown,
And frosts and shortening days portend
The aged year is at an end.

NAME:

Double creeping buttercup
(*Ranunculus repens*
'Pleniflorus')

HEIGHT:

30 to 60 cm (1 to 2 feet)

HARDY TO:

Zone 3

EXPOSURE:

Full sun to part shade

BLOOMING PERIOD:

Late spring to mid-summer

SOIL:

Average garden soil; plants
spread more prolifically
under moist conditions

COMPANIONS:

Associates well with
columbine (*Aquilegia spp.*
and cvs.), Dame's rocket
(*Hesperis matronalis*), and
late tulips (*Tulipa spp.*). Also
effective under shrubs

SPECIAL NOTES:

Seldom bothered by insects
or disease, the only maintenance likely to be required
is to cut back runners if they
outgrow their bounds.

double creeping buttercup

ranunculus repens 'pleniflorus'

The double creeping buttercup is not a native plant, but can you even begin to imagine a meadow garden without it? Shakespeare certainly couldn't:

When daisies pied and violets blue,
And lady-smocks, all silver-white,
And cuckoo-buds of yellow hue
Do paint the meadows with delight
    (Love's Labour's Lost, *Act V, Sc. ii*)

In Shakespeare's day, buttercups were known as "cuckoo-buds" or "crowfoot" — in fact the name "buttercup" doesn't appear in print until the middle of the eighteenth century. However, two double forms of buttercup were grown in English gardens when John Gerard (1545–1612) wrote his famous *Herball* in 1597. He cultivated both *Ranunculus repens* 'Pleniflorus' and the tall double buttercup *R. acris* 'Flore Pleno'. He collected the latter variety in a field next to Shakespeare's Globe Theatre, so it is hardly surprising that the playwright was familiar with the plant. The double creeping buttercup was introduced into London gardens at about the same time by "a curious gentleman in the fetching foorth of simples, Master Thomas Hesketh, who found it growing wild in Lancashire."

It would appear from these early accounts that the double forms of *Ranunculus* are the result of natural genetic mutations that cause the number of petals to double or triple spontaneously; another example of this phenomenon can be observed in the naturally occurring double forms of our native bloodroot (*Sanguinaria canadensis*).

The *Ranunculus* genus is a large one, containing about four hundred separate species. Unfortunately, many of the more ornamental types such as the Persian buttercup (*Ranunculus asiaticus*), the bulbous buttercup (*R. bulbosus*), and the double Constantinople buttercup (*R. constantinopolitanus* 'Plenus') are only reliably hardy to Zone 7. Luckily for the rest of us, *Ranunculus repens* 'Pleniflorus' (hardy to Zone 3) will fit the buttercup bill splendidly, providing a succession of glossy yellow flowers 1.5 to 2 cm (½ to ¾ inch) across, from early to mid-summer.

Many gardeners are concerned that the hardier species of buttercup will become too aggressive and weedy, and indeed, single-flowered varieties of both *Ranunculus acris* and *R. repens* should be avoided, although the double forms are much more well-behaved.

Seen here emerging from a clump of meadow cranesbill foliage (Geranium pratense 'Striatum'), the double creeping buttercup (Ranunculus repens 'Pleniflorus') loves to insinuate itself among other flowering plants. Once the double buttercup has faded, the Geranium takes over, and after it has finished blooming, yarrow hybrids (e.g., Achillea millefolium 'Cerise Queen') add colour for the remainder of the summer.

The other point to bear in mind is that most buttercups like moist soil conditions and plenty of sunshine, so to prevent them from becoming overly abundant, simply grow them in the drier areas of your meadow garden or under the half shade cast by taller perennials and shrubs.

I like the double creeping buttercup for more than just its intricate golden flowers; it's also a consummate fraternizer, and is invariably seen to best advantage when rubbing shoulders with other meadow garden habitués. Arising from a central tuft of shiny green foliage, each plant begins to send out stolons (runners) away from the central crown. At

each node (or bud) on the runner, a small plant develops, and providing the runner is in contact with the soil, each individual new plant will quickly take root. These runners insinuate themselves among the foliage of nearby plants and efficiently cover bare soil, making it the perfect plant for the meadow garden, or as Graham Stuart Thomas called it "a showy carpeter."

In spite of being called creeping, *Ranunculus repens* 'Pleniflorus' sends up flowering spikes to a height of between 30 and 60 cm (1 and 2 feet), so providing it's grown with other mid-sized plants, the blooms will never be concealed. I like to grow it with other equally assertive plants such as meadow cranesbill (*Geranium pratense* 'Striatum') and yarrow cultivars (*Achillea* cvs.), and then leave them to battle it out together.

Once flowering has finished, I generally assess the area, and any plants I don't want are removed. Runners and the immature plants they produce are easy to pull up if the playing field should begin to look a little uneven. It's actually a job I relish since you can pull up a tremendous amount of greenery with virtually no effort. Plants that I intend to keep are sheared back close to ground level to prevent self-seeding and to produce fresh green foliage.

If you're feeling a bit insecure about installing a plant that your neighbours might think is a weed on par with dandelions, take courage from Margery Fish's bold words, and quote her to your detractors if necessary: "I wonder why we fuss about double flowers, because on the whole I don't think they compare with the single-flowered forms. But many of them have the charm of the unusual. I wouldn't cherish an ordinary butter-cup, however magnificent a specimen, but I check regularly to see that no zealous friend has removed my precious double buttercups which look just like common weeds when not in flower."

Sometimes natural genetic mutations generate extra petals, as is the case with the double creeping buttercup (Ranunculus repens 'Pleniflorus') but they can also produce variations in colour. Pictured here is a white "mutant" form of the pale purple coneflower (Echinacea pallida), flanked by spiderwort (Tradescantia ohiensis).

NAME:
Michaelmas daisy
(*Aster spp.*)
HEIGHT:
1.2 to 1.5 m (4 to 5 feet)
HARDY TO:
Zone 2 or 3
EXPOSURE:
Full to part sun
BLOOMING PERIOD:
Late summer to late
autumn
SOIL:
Ordinary to lean garden soil
COMPANIONS:
Lovely in conjunction with
Sedum 'Herbstfreude' (syn.
S. 'Autumn Joy'), or small
shrubs such as butterfly
bush (*Buddleja davidii* and
cvs.) and blue mist shrub
(*Caryopteris × clandonensis*)
SPECIAL NOTES:
Like chrysanthemums
(*Dendranthema spp.*) and
poinsettias (*Euphorbia
pulcherrima*), fall asters
won't initiate flowering
until the shorter days of
autumn arrive, a process
known as photoperiodism.

michaelmas daisy

aster spp.

The genus *Aster* belongs to the Asteraceae (or daisy) family, which until recently was known as the Compositae family. The daisy clan is one of the largest in the plant kingdom, containing 1,300 genera, 21,000 individual species, and innumerable cultivars, in total making up fully one-tenth of the world's flowering plants.

The *Aster* genus itself contains more than 250 species, and while some are native to Eurasia, and several to South Africa and South America, the vast majority are indigenous to North America. Most gardeners consider autumn-blooming asters (or Michaelmas daisies) to be essential to any garden scheme since they bloom late in the season at a time when most other perennials have closed up shop for the year. The two most important species of these autumn-blooming asters are *Aster novi-belgii* (New York aster) and *A. novae-angliae* (New England aster).

With more cultivars to its credit than any other *Aster,* the species *Novi-belgii* was first described in 1687 by Paul Hermann, a German botanist teaching at a Dutch university. The seeds for the plants that Hermann cultivated were collected in what is now Manhattan — originally a Dutch colony known as New Amsterdam. Although it had been held by the British since 1664 and re-named New York, at no time was the area known as New Belgium (*Novi-belgii*), so we must assume that Novi-belgii was about as close as Hermann could come to a Latinized form of New Netherlands.

Native to the eastern seaboard from Newfoundland south and hardy to Zone 3, plants may grow as tall as 1.2 m (4 feet) and bear masses of violet flowers about 6 cm (2 inches) across from early to late autumn. New York asters prefer a full sun location, but are completely adaptable when it comes to soil. I find that plants seem to naturally gravitate toward areas with poor soil, so I have long since given up any notion of wasting precious compost on these tough guys. I've already mentioned that seedlings of *Aster novi-belgii* have colonized several cracks in my driveway and flagstone walkway (a domicile they share with *Verbena bonariensis, Aquilegia,* and sweet alyssum), the result of spontaneous crosses

*Even in naturalized meadows,
plants always look their best
when they are arranged in clumps.
Pictured here (l to r) is beebalm
(Monarda didyma), black-eyed
Susan (Rudbeckia hirta),
blazingstar (Liatris spicata),
and purple coneflower
(Echinacea purpurea).*

Many of the *Aster novi-belgii* cultivars available today are the result of intensive British breeding during the 1950s. Keep a lookout for any of the following no-nonsense New York asters, then let them get down to the serious business of cross-pollinating.

CULTIVAR NAME	INTRODUCED	COLOUR
'Ada Ballard'	1952	Lilac-blue
'Alice Haslam'	1958	Pale red
'Apple Blossom'	1952	Pale pink
'Boningale White'	1963	White
'Chequers'	1953	Rich violet
'Crimson Brocade'	1950	Purple-red
'Ernest Ballard'	1950	Purple-pink
'Eventide'	1950	Lavender-blue
'Fellowship'	1955	Pale pink
'Freda Ballard'	1959	Purple-red
'Lady in Blue'	1955	Lavender-blue
'Lassie'	1955	Pale pink
'Marie Ballard'	1955	Lavender-blue
'Mount Everest'	pre-1930	White
'Niobe'	pre-1935	White
'Patricia Ballard'	1957	Mauve-pink
'Peace'	1946	Lilac
'Percy Thrower'	1958	Lavender-blue
'Professor Anton Kippenberg'	1949	Lavender-blue
'Rosenwichtel'	1969	Deep pink
'Royal Ruby' (syn. 'Jenny')	1966	Purple-red
'Schneekissen' (syn. 'Snowcushion')	1954	White
'Snowsprite'	pre-1935	White
'The Cardinal'	pre-1950	Purple-pink
'Winston S. Churchill'	1950	Purple-red

between several named cultivars located in other areas of the garden.

All in all, I think that this is the easiest way to get autumn asters to spread around your garden. I've never had much luck growing asters from seed; they seem to prefer to carry out this operation on their own, and do so much more efficiently when left to their own devices. By purchasing several of the widely available cultivars of *Aster novi-belgii* (there are about three hundred currently in commerce world-wide), you will set yourself up with a perfect mini breeding factory. Leave autumn seed heads in place until after the first hard frosts, and after cutting them back, give the spent flower heads a sharp whack on the soil surface to release any recalcitrant seeds. Mother Nature will do the rest.

New York asters are drought tolerant in spite of being rather shallowly rooted. Within one year, a spreading, woody rootstock will develop, replete with stoloniferous shoots that will produce new plants at their tips (much like a strawberry runner), making the propagation of new plants even easier. Asters can also be divided every few years (in early spring) to increase your stock of named cultivars, since seedlings rarely come true to type.

In a casual meadow setting, staking plants should never be undertaken, and it's easy to avoid this tiresome task. In mid to late June, I cut my asters back from between one-half to two-thirds of their current height. This achieves three goals: It reduces the ultimate stature of the plant by as much as 45 cm (18 inches), it encourages a bushier habit, and it delays bloom for ten to fourteen days, extending the flowering season well into autumn.

Although *Aster novi-belgii* and *A. novae-angliae* weren't introduced to Britain until 1710, Philip Miller was acutely aware of the attributes of both of them. In the 1754 edition of *The Gardeners Dictionary* he writes, "In large Wildernesses they are very good to fill up Vacancies, and the Flowers are very proper to adorn Halls and Chimneys; and as they come at a Season when few better Flowers appear, are the more valuable."

William Robinson was also an enthusiastic supporter: "There is a quiet beauty about the more select *Asters*, which is charming in the autumn days, and their variety of colour, of form, and of bud and blossom is delightful. Even where not introduced into

Can you spot the bumblebee? An important late-season pollen source, these New York asters (Aster novi-belgii) grow in the cracks of my driveway (which clearly needs mending). A master of the understatement, William Robinson put it best when he wrote, "Nothing can be more easy to cultivate."

the flower garden, they should always be grown for cutting; and they are excellent for forming bold groups to cover the bare ground among newly-planted shrubs. Nothing can be more easy to cultivate."

Less given to the horticultural promiscuity that pervades the rest of the genus is *Aster novae-angliae:* the chaste New England aster. It has a much wider distribution than *Aster novi-belgii*, its natural range stretches from Quebec west to Saskatchewan, and it is slightly hardier (to Zone 2). Although many fewer cultivars have been developed from *Aster novae-angliae* than from *A. novi-belgii*, it tends to be longer lived and is also less troubled by sporadic mildew outbreaks.

The cultural requirements for New England asters are virtually the same as for New York asters, and in fact, many gardeners aren't altogether certain which of the two they're actually growing since the similarities far outweigh the differences. Generally speaking, left unpruned in June, New England asters are slightly taller plants (to 1.5 m / 5 feet) with marginally smaller flowers (to 5 cm / 2 inches).

For gardeners who crave a shorter plant (height to 70 cm / 28 inches) without having to prune in June, there is *Aster × frikartii*, the result of crossing the Italian *Aster amellus* with the Himalayan *Aster thomsonii*. Neither natural nor native, this is nevertheless a useful plant with an exceptionally long period of bloom, often extending from midsummer to mid-autumn, although it is only reliably hardy to Zone 5.

Introduced in 1918 by the Swiss nurseryman Frikart, the first hybrids of *Aster × frikartii* were named after three famous mountain peaks: 'Eiger', 'Jungfrau', and 'Monch', all of which are still available, although 'Monch' is by far the finest and most popular. A plantsman not given to overstatement, Graham Stuart Thomas rhapsodizes, "'Monch' is not only the finest perennial aster; it is one of the six best plants, and should be in every garden. (Please do not ask for the names of the other five.)" So consider yourself told!

Although fewer in number, there are still plenty of excellent *Aster novae-angliae* cultivars available to get your meadow garden off to a great start:

CULTIVAR NAME	INTRODUCED	COLOUR
'Andenken an Alma Potschke'	1969	Cerise-pink
'Barr's Pink'	1920	Rosy lilac-pink
'Crimson Beauty'	1920	Purple-red
'Harrington's Pink'	1943	Rose-pink
'Herbstschnee' (syn. 'Autumn Snow')	1981	White
'Lou Williams'	1995	Purple-red
'Purple Dome'	1990	Violet-purple
'Rosa Sieger'	1971	Rose-pink
'Rubinschatz'	1960	Purple-pink
'Septemberrubin' (syn. 'September Ruby')	1951	Purple-red

The ripe, black seed heads of purple coneflower (Echinacea purpurea) represent a valuable autumn food source for migrating birds, and they could never be accused of detracting from the quiet beauty of a clump of New England asters (Aster novae-angliae).

NAME:
Purple coneflower
(*Echinacea purpurea*)
HEIGHT:
1.0 to 1.5 m (3 to 5 feet)
HARDY:
From Zones 3 to 9
EXPOSURE:
Full sun to part shade
BLOOMING PERIOD:
Late summer to late
autumn
SOIL:
Prefers lean, unamended
soil
COMPANIONS:
Associates well with bee-
balm (*Monarda spp.*), garden
phlox (*Phlox paniculata*),
and mountain mint
(*Pycnanthemum virginianum*).
They're often planted in
conjunction with yellow
coneflowers (*Ratibida* and
Rudbeckia spp.), but I find
the foliage and flower
forms too similar, not to
mention the jarring colour
combo (purple and yellow).
SPECIAL NOTES:
After the goldfinches have
eaten their fill, seed heads
can be removed to prevent
excessive self-seeding.

purple coneflower

echinacea spp.

Echinacea is now almost as well known as aspirin, and although I'm not particularly given to herbal remedies, I must admit I reach for the *Echinacea* capsules whenever I feel a cold coming on. Placebo effect aside, I'm certain it's beneficial, and why not? Many of the old herbal remedies have proven to be efficacious for a panorama of ailments, although most of us have become such sceptical consumers that we quite rightly want to read about it in *The Lancet* or *The American Journal of Medicine* before we actually ingest it. In any case, I'll confine my comments to purple coneflower's merit as a garden plant, rather than as a herbal remedy.

Echinacea purpurea was one of the first perennial plants I introduced to my garden, and many years later I can't begin to imagine autumn without it. As one sagacious gardener recently pointed out to me, "Plan for your garden to be in bloom during August and September — spring and summer will take care of themselves," and this is very apt advice. *Echinacea* tends to grow best east of the Rockies, although I've seen some very good stands in the Vancouver area. Nevertheless, all species of *Echinacea* prefer hot, dry conditions, making it an excellent choice for the meadow garden.

As is so often the case, although *Echinacea* grows better in North America than in Europe (too much rain coupled with insufficient heat), most of the efforts to develop new cultivars and improved strains have been concentrated in Britain, and to a lesser degree, in Germany.

How the plant got to Europe in the first place is another story. One of the most successful importers of plants from the Virginian colonies to England was Henry Compton, Bishop of London, member of the Temple Coffee House Botanists' Club, and more importantly, head of the Church for the American Colonies. This last posting afforded him so many opportunities to cram his Fulham Palace garden full of newly discovered plants from North America that he suffered stinging pangs of guilt at the end of his life over his lavish expenditures.

In due course, he sent out a young missionary who had shown botanical promise while still an undergrad at Oxford: John Banister (1654–92). Banister arrived in Virginia in 1678 and immediately began sending seeds back to the Oxford Botanic Garden, among them seeds for *Echinacea*

Looking a little like a floral squid emerging from the depths, pale purple coneflower (Echinacea pallida) is likely the best choice for gardeners in the prairies.

Obedient plant (Physostegia virginiana) is just one of many species that the ill-fated John Banister sent back to England from the Virginian colonies. The common name alludes to the fact that each individual flower has a malleable, "hinged" stalk, so that blooms remain fixed in position when they are moved.

purpurea, which at the time was classified as a member of the *Rudbeckia* genus. Banister had intended to write "a more particular Account of the Plants of this country: viz. such as are Cultivated and manured, or Wild and spontaneous," but this was not to be, owing to his early death, the result of a tumble ("he fell from the rocks, and perished") during a plant-finding expedition. Now that's dedication!

I won't dwell on the cultural requirements of *Echinacea,* because they are few. Plants prefer a full sun location, but will also bloom quite satisfactorily in partly shaded conditions. While some writers assert that *Echinacea* flops if given any shade at all, and will subsequently require staking, this just isn't the case. The only thing that will make plants fall over (and at the same time reduce bloom) is if they are grown in a rich soil. Save your compost and leaf mould for a plant that will appreciate it. *Echinacea spp.* thrive on a lean diet, so extensive soil amendment or auxiliary nutrient sources are strictly *verboten.*

To extend the blooming season, selected clumps of *Echinacea* may be reduced by half their height in early summer (exactly the same procedure as with fall-blooming *Aster spp.*). This will retard their blooming season by several weeks, while at the same time encouraging a bushy habit on slightly shorter plants.

In spite of the fact that Echinacea purpurea *contains compounds that are toxic to houseflies and mosquitoes, its nectar is an important food source for butterflies, and in the autumn, its seeds provide an essential source of fuel for migrating birds. Pictured here with a red admiral butterfly, it is also much esteemed by monarch, swallowtail, mourning cloak, and fritillary butterflies.*

Our old pal Philip Miller grew *Echinacea purpurea* shortly after it was introduced to England, although in the 1754 edition of *The Gardeners Dictionary* it was included with the *Rudbeckia* genus, the common name being given as "American sunflower with purple rays." He went on to say that "as it is a scarce Plant, it is generally sold at a good Price by those who deal in curious Plants."

The reason that plants were so expensive in Miller's day is primarily due to location: exposed to cool, moist British summers, they rarely set much seed. However in most of North America the problem is the reverse, and if all the seed heads are left in place, the second generation will undoubtedly prove too successful for many gardeners. As with most things in life, the solution lies in a compromise. After the first flush of flowers (which will prove irresistible to butterflies), I try to deadhead as many spent blooms as I can. This first

Surely a glimpse of the Elysian fields—pale purple coneflower (Echinacea pallida) for as far as the eye can see, coupled with an exquisite "Big Sky."

flowering will be followed by an equally prolific second flush of flowers, and it is these late bloomers that I leave in place. An important food source for goldfinches and migrating birds, whatever seed heads haven't been picked clean by late autumn are then cut back to prevent a glut of seedlings the following spring. Using this method, you can attract wildlife to your meadow garden without finding yourself in the midst of an *Echinacea* monoculture after just a few seasons.

While most *Echinacea* species will thrive in most of North America, as a general rule, *E. purpurea* is the best choice for gardeners in the Northeast. If you live in the prairies, *Echinacea angustifolia* or *E. pallida* will likely perform the best for you. Gardeners in the Pacific Northwest should set their sights on some of the *Echinacea purpurea* cultivars developed in Britain and Germany that have established themselves as proven winners in cool, moist climates. Keep an eye out for 'Bravado', 'Finale White', 'Leuchstern', 'Magnus', 'Robert Bloom', and 'White Swan'.

In addition to its other attributes, purple coneflower contains a compound that is toxic to houseflies and mosquitoes, and is currently being investigated as a potential insect deterrent. Catherine Parr Traill certainly kept an open mind on such matters: "Many splendid species of the Cone-flower are to be found on the wide-spread prairies of the West, where their brilliant starry flowers are mingled with many a gay blossom known only to the wild Indian hunter, and the herb-seeking Medicine-men of the native tribes, who know their medicinal and healing qualities. One tall, purple-rayed species (*Echinacea purpurea*) is very handsome."

queen of the prairie

filipendula rubra

All of the filipendulas are members of the Rosaceae (Rose) family, and at one time or another most species have been included in the closely related *Spiraea* genus. The name *Filipendula* is derived from the Latin *filium* (a thread) and *pendulus* (hanging), since the tuberous roots of some species hang together with what look like threads. Most garden-worthy species hail from Japan and the Kamchatka Peninsula, as well as two more from Eurasia, but to my mind, the cream of the crop is our native *Filipendula rubra*.

Hardy from Zones 3 to 9 and towering above the competition at 2.5 m (8 feet), the aptly named Queen of the prairie produces crowded corymbs (or clusters) of fragrant peach-pink flowers from early to mid-summer, which look for all the world like pink cotton candy. At its best in a full sun location, Queen of the prairie is a majestic, regal plant by anyone's standards.

After it flowers, I usually remove the spent blooms since they aren't particularly attractive, and enough new plants will be produced from the spreading roots that I don't need extra seedlings. Unlike some of the other plants we've been discussing, the height of Queen of the prairie cannot be curtailed by means of a mid-June pruning. Plants that are cut back will fail to flower, and even assiduous deadheading (post-bloom) will fail to induce the Queen to produce a second flush of buds. This being the case, if the remaining stalks of *Filipendula rubra* begin to look bedraggled by late summer, I simply cut them back to their base, where they will form an attractive low mound of fresh new leaves.

In the wild, Queen of the prairie tends to inhabit wet meadows, so the conventional wisdom runs that home gardeners should attempt to reproduce these same conditions. Nothing could be farther from the truth: When grown in very rich soil coupled with consistent moisture, *Filipendula rubra* will transform itself from a Queen into a Villainess before your very eyes. Feeling much too much at home, *Filipendula rubra* can run riot when cultivated under these conditions and may quickly form a dense thicket. The solution, then, is to grow this plant in average meadow conditions, which is to say, on the dry side. Treated this way, Queen of the prairie will spread, but it will never become invasive.

As if to reinforce the point, Queen of the prairie is native to the Great Lakes states, where average rainfalls are not particularly high, so save the wet areas of your garden for plants that really demand extra moisture in order to survive. Interestingly, like the

---

NAME:
Queen of the prairie
(*Filipendula rubra*)
HEIGHT:
2.5 m (8 feet)
HARDY TO:
Zone 3
EXPOSURE:
Full sun
BLOOMING PERIOD:
Early to mid-summer
SOIL:
Average garden soil. Avoid wet soils, which will cause rampant, spreading growth.
COMPANIONS:
For a completely over-the-top floral display, plant Queen of the prairie with bellflowers (*Campanula spp.* and cvs.) and delphiniums (*Delphinium spp.* and cvs.)
SPECIAL NOTES:
In addition to the species form, there is one widely available cultivar called 'Venusta', which is sometimes offered under the erroneous names 'Magnifica' or 'Venusta Magnifica'.

closely related European Queen of the meadow (*Filipendula ulmaria*), *F. rubra* is thought to contain the chemical forerunners of aspirin (salicylic acid), and certainly there is no doubt that the Fox Indians (Wisconsin) used an extract of the root to treat heart problems.

Although this plant will spread (and let's remember, we want it to!), it does so in a very accommodating way, sending up a single spike here, another there, so that it is possible to insinuate several floral layers beneath the area in which it is growing. Because these random spikes rarely disturb nearby plants, I grow Queen of the prairie with our native blue fleabane (*Erigeron speciosus*) and *Paeonia* × *smouthii* for a floral mid-story, which in turn is grounded with low-growing alpine forget-me-nots (*Myosotis alpestris*) and heartsease (*Viola tricolor*). Self-seeded purple morning glories (*Convolvulus* 'Star of Yelta') complete the picture as they invariably seek out, and then scramble up, the tall sturdy stems of *Filipendula rubra*.

Filipendula rubra was introduced to Britain in 1765 but for some reason didn't attract much comment from the venerable old garden writers. However Graham Stuart Thomas appears to have atoned for this untoward neglect when he comments: "The Queen of the Prairie can indeed queen it over any herbaceous plant of her season, and from her great height can look down on other filipendulas. For many years the Old Garden at Hidcote, Gloucestershire, has been graced by this fine plant." Since Hidcote Manor is undoubtedly the gardening equivalent of Buckingham Palace, I suppose we must congratulate our expatriate Queen on establishing herself in such stately surroundings.

Looking like a swirl of pink cotton candy, Queen of the prairie (Filipendula rubra) is indeed capable of lording it over her more diminutive subjects. It's hardy from Zones 3 to 9 and native to the Great Lakes region; it's wise to grow this Filipendula in the drier areas of your naturalized meadow, since given sufficient moisture, Her Majesty may be tempted to stage a botanical insurrection.

Although I consider *Filipendula rubra* to be the Belle of the Ball, there are also several non-native species that are well-suited to natural meadow gardens:

NAME	HARDY TO ZONE
Dropwort (*F. vulgaris* [syn. *F. hexapetala*])	4
Japanese meadowsweet (*F. purpurea*)	4
Kamchatka meadowsweet (*Filipendula kamtschatica*)	3
Queen of the meadow (*F. ulmaria* [syn. *Spiraea ulmaria*])	3
Siberian meadowsweet (*F. palmata* (syn. *Spiraea palmata*)	2

NAME:
Willow blue star
(*Amsonia tabernaemontana*)
HEIGHT:
60 cm (2 feet)
HARDY TO:
Zone 3
EXPOSURE:
Performs best in full sun,
will tolerate partial shade
BLOOMING PERIOD:
Late spring to early summer
SOIL:
Average garden soil, avoid
water-logged conditions
COMPANIONS:
Excellent with other no-
fuss perennials, particularly
those with contrasting leaf
shapes such as Lady's
mantle (*Alchemilla mollis*),
meadow rue (*Thalictrum spp.*),
and daylilies (*Hemerocallis
spp.* and cvs.)
SPECIAL NOTES:
Don't overlook willow blue
star's colourful autumn
foliage, which associates
well with Michaelmas
daisies (*Aster novi-belgii*)
and hardy chrysanthemums
(*Dendranthema spp.* and cvs.).

willow blue star

amsonia tabernaemontana

There is no doubt in my mind that by the end of the twenty-first century, willow blue star will be as well-known a perennial plant as oriental poppies or delphiniums are at the beginning of it. In short, this is a plant that has everything going for it — all it lacks is a good publicist.

Native to eastern North America from New Jersey and the Great Lakes states to as far south as Texas, willow blue star is the hardiest (Zones 3 to 9) of the several *Amsonia spp.* under cultivation. In spite of the fact that specimens of willow blue star were sent from Virginia to Britain as early as 1759, it is rarely seen in European gardens. The genus is named in honour of a seventeenth-century Virginian physician, Dr. Charles Amson, while the species is named for Jakob Theodore von Bergzabern (d. 1590), a professor of botany at Heidelberg University who "Latinized" his name to the mellifluous *Tabernaemontanus.*

Blooming from late spring to early summer, willow blue star produces dense panicles (or clusters) of pale blue flowers, with each individual flower measuring 1 to 2 cm (½ to ¾ inch) across. Although willow blue star is late to show in the spring, once the green shoots emerge from its woody rootstock, growth is swift, reaching a maximum height of about 60 cm (2 feet) just as the buds are breaking. I like to combine the stately, steely blue flowers with rambunctious lupines (*Lupinus* cvs.), which would doubtless look like a Mardi Gras float without the restraining influence of the *Amsonia.*

Willow blue star has virtually no disease or insect pests, and while some gardeners recommend that it be grown in moist soil, I grow mine in an extremely dry section of the garden, and it has never flagged from lack of water. *Amsonia tabernaemontana* is also very cooperative when it comes to self-seeding. After flowering, slim pods that look like anorexic peas develop, which in turn slowly release their seeds in the autumn. Many of these seeds will germinate the following spring, although the young seedlings may require transplanting as

I like to combine willow blue star (Amsonia tabernaemontana) with garish lupines (Lupinus 'Band of Nobles' series) in a dry, sunny section of my garden. Amsonia seedlings tend to grow too close to parent plants and should be transplanted once they reach a height of 10 cm (4 inches). All blue stars contain a milky sap that may irritate sensitive skins.

they tend to grow within the canopy of the parent plant, which can ultimately lead to overcrowded colonies.

Willow blue star will eventually form quite a hefty clump, as much as 50 cm (20 inches) across, so plants should be spaced accordingly when they are installed. If you don't want new seedlings, it's best to deadhead the plants once flowering has ended. Plants tend to have a naturally rounded form, and this should be encouraged during the deadheading process. Plants may be cut back up to 50 percent of their original height, but try to leave stems at the centre of the plant a little longer, and cut back outer stems more severely. This will reinforce a mounded shape, while at the same time promoting a bushier habit. As a final bonus, the foliage of willow blue star (which indeed resembles the leaves of willow trees) will turn a stunning yellow-apricot colour in autumn.

In spite of willow blue star being little known in Europe, Margery Fish grew *Amsonia tabernaemontana* (var. *salicifolia*) and praised it for its "quiet charm," although Graham Stuart Thomas appears to have preferred the closely related Greco-Turkish *A. orientalis* (syn. *Rhazya orientalis*). In addition to willow blue star, several other members of the *Amsonia* family merit consideration for the naturalized meadow garden:

Arkansas blue star (*Amsonia hubrectii*) Zones 4 to 9

Blue milkweed (*Amsonia ciliata*) Zones 5 to 9

Leatherleaf blue star (*Amsonia illustris*) Zones 5 to 9

Louisiana blue star (*Amsonia ludoviciana*) Zones 6 to 9

the damp
garden

Contrary to what many people may think,
there are hundreds if not thousands of
hardy plants that will appreciate the extra
moisture of the damp garden, enabling homeowners to expand their horticultural horizons
significantly. Resist the urge to drain these
distinctive pockets, and instead endeavour
to preserve their natural character.

Most gardeners have at least one spot in their garden where water collects — perhaps because the land itself is low-lying, or there are underground springs in the area that occasionally bubble to the surface, or perhaps it is something as simple as run-off from eaves trough downspouts. Whatever the reason, the solution will always be the same: to plant species that thrive in these wetter than average conditions.

Importing vast quantities of sand and gravel or laying weeping tiles to increase drainage is not the approach the natural gardener will take. Of course, damp gardens can be created and ponds installed, but the emphasis in the naturalized garden will always be to work with existing conditions without altering the natural character of the area in question.

The same basic principles of naturalization apply to the damp garden as to woodland or meadow gardens. You can improve the soil with compost and other sources of organic matter, but beyond plant installation and some basic seasonal maintenance, the naturalized damp garden should largely take care of itself. Plants should be selected for their ability to withstand waterlogged conditions, to spread without becoming invasive, and to resist insects and diseases.

Damp gardens can either be sunny or shady, but the majority of gardeners will usually find that wet or boggy sites are somewhat lacking in woody plant material, so one of the first orders of business will be to select some permanent trees and shrubs that will give your damp garden solid structure and form. Across most of North America, boggy sites are usually quite wet in the spring, but tend to gradually dry out during the heat of summer. In the autumn with the return of the rains and cooler temperatures, these areas often begin to once again fill up with water. Many European bog plants are unable to cope with these seasonal fluctuations since they require consistent moisture throughout the growing season, from early spring to late autumn. Fortunately for us, many of our native plants are well adapted to our alternating cycle of wet / dry / wet soil, making them much more able to withstand the vagaries of our North American climate.

While most gardeners won't have the ultimate luxury of actually having a natural pond or stream running through their property, the higher moisture levels present in the damp garden will nevertheless attract a great deal of wildlife.

Insects depend on ready sources of water when they go about raising their families, and don't forget that ninety-five percent of all insects are beneficial in one way or another, so it's best to adopt a "live and let live" attitude. Many gardeners are uncertain about whether a given insect is beneficial or not, so set yourself up with an insect identification or field guide, so you can become familiar with the various caterpillars, bugs, beetles, and spiders that will assist you in your gardening chores.

Many trees are well suited to the water-saturated conditions of the damp garden. They provide food and shelter for wildlife, they give the garden structure (or "bones," as landscapers are fond of saying), and they provide shade. All of the following native species will feel perfectly at home in the naturalized damp garden, and are tolerant of soils with poor drainage.

NAME	HARDY TO ZONE	NAME	HARDY TO ZONE
Ash		**Other Trees**	
Black ash (*Fraxinus nigra*)	2	American planetree (*Platanus occidentalis*)	4
Blue ash (*Fraxinus quadrangulata*)	5	American sweetgum (*Liquidamber styraciflua*)	6
Green ash (*Fraxinus pennsylvanica lanceolata*)	2	American yellow wood (*Cladrastis lutea*)	3
Buckeye		Balsam fir (*Abies balsamea*)	2
Ohio buckeye (*Aesculus glabra*)	4	Bigtooth aspen (*Populus grandidentat*)	3
Yellow buckeye (*Aesculus flava* [syn. A. octandra])	4	Black gum (*Nyssa sylvatica*)	5
Hickory		Black spruce (*Picea mariana*)	2
Bitternut hickory (*Carya cordiformis*)	4	Canada hemlock (*Tsuga canadensis*)	3
Shagbark hickory (*Carya ovata*)	4	Common bald cypress (*Taxodium disticum*)	5
Maple		Common hackberry (*Celtis occidentalis*)	3
Red maple (*Acer rubrum*)	3	Common honeylocust (*Gleditsia tricanthos*)	4
Silver maple (*Acer saccharinum*)	3	Eastern arborvitae (*Thuja occidentalis*)	2
Oak		Eastern larch (*Larix laricina*)	2
Bur oak (*Quercus macrocarpa*)	2	Eastern poplar (*Populus deltoides*)	3
Pin oak (*Quercus palustris*)	5	Hazel alder (*Alnus rugosa*)	2
Swamp white oak (*Quercus bicolor*)	4	Kentucky coffeetree (*Gymnocladus dioicus*)	5
Willow		Northern catalpa (*Catalpa speciosa*)	5
Bebb willow (*Salix bebbiana*)	2	Quaking aspen (*Populus tremuloides*)	2
Black willow (*Salix nigra*)	3	River birch (*Betula nigra*)	5
Peachleaf willow (*Salix amygdaloides*)	3	Showy mountain ash (*Sorbus decora*)	2
Pussy willow (*Salix discolor*)	2		

Shrubs provide an important intermediate level between tall trees and herbaceous plants. Any of the following native species will thrive in wet, poorly drained soils:

NAME	HARDY TO ZONE	NAME	HARDY TO ZONE
Chokeberry		American red raspberry (*Rubus strigosis*)	2
Black chokeberry (*Aronia melanocarpa*)	3	Bog kalmia (*Kalmia polifolia*)	2
Red chokeberry (*Aronia arbutifolia*)	4	Bogrosemary andromeda (*Andromeda polifolia*)	2
Dogwood		Canadian elder (*Sambucus canadensis*)	3
Bunchberry (*Cornus canadensis*)	2	Common buttonbush (*Cephalanthus occidentalis*)	4
Redosier dogwood (*Cornus stolonifera*)	2	Common ninebark (*Physocarpus opulifolius*)	2
Silky dogwood (*Cornus amomum*)	4	Dusty zenobia (*Zenobia pulverulenta*)	6
Rhododendron		Dwarf fothergilla (*Fothergilla gardeni*)	6
Swamp azalea (*Rhododendron viscosum*)	4	Eastern baccharis (*Baccharis halimifolia*)	4
Sweet azalea (*Rhododendron arborescens*)	4	He-huckleberry (*Lyonia ligustrina*)	5
Spiraea		Indigobush amorpha (*Amorpha fruticosa*)	3
Hardhack spiraea (*Spiraea tomentosa*)	4	Leather-leaf (*Chamaedaphne calyculata*)	2
Narrowleaf meadowsweet (*Spiraea alba*)	3	Lowbush blueberry (*Vaccinium angustifolium*)	2
More Shrubs		Summersweet clethra (*Clethra alnifolia*)	4
American black currant (*Ribes americanum*)	3	Virginia sweetspire (*Itea virginica*)	5
American cyrilla (*Cyrilla racemiflora*)	6		

In turn, these insects will attract other forms of beneficial wildlife to your garden. Toads will soon appear, ready to snatch up flying insects, birds will cherish your dawn to dusk smorgasbord, and ladybird larvae will grow fat on local aphids. All in all, a much more pastoral, sustainable approach than to reach for a pressurized can of insecticide!

Gardeners fortunate enough to have a stream or pond as part of their damp garden can look forward to plenty of visitors. Insects, birds, small mammals, amphibians, and reptiles will relish the easy access to a reliable source of water. And if you're lucky, you too can sport frog-adorned lily pads!

NAME:

Cowslip, primrose
(*Primula spp.*)

HEIGHT:

20 to 25 cm (8 to 10 inches)

HARDY TO:

Zones 3 to 4

EXPOSURE:

Both cowslips and
primroses appreciate
partly shaded conditions
in warmer zones, but
require more sunshine
in cooler areas.

BLOOMING PERIOD:

Early to late spring

SOIL:

Rich soil with plenty of
organic matter and ample
moisture. Plants will go
dormant in regions where
summers are particularly
hot and dry.

COMPANIONS:

I like to grow many vari-
eties of *Primula* together
fairly close to the house for
a spectacular springtime
display. Once they have
faded, Japanese painted
ferns (*Athyrium niponicum*
var. *pictum*) take over, as do
foxgloves (*Digitalis purpurea*)
and purple perilla (*Perilla
frutescens* var. *crispa*).

cowslip, primrose

primula spp.

I've always maintained that if I could only grow one genus, it would be *Primula*. Lately I've taken to qualifying this as "If I could only grow one *spring-blooming* genus, it would be…" Otherwise it would all be over for me by the end of May!

The *Primula* genus comprises about 425 species, over half of which are native to the Himalayas. North America can boast twenty indigenous species, most of them concentrated on the west coast of the continent. However, the two types that I recommend for damp gardens are neither indigenous nor alpine. The cowslip (*Primula veris*) and the primrose (*P. vulgaris*) are generally deemed to be quintessentially English flowers, although their natural range stretches across much of Eurasia.

the cowslip

The names "primrose" and *Primula* are derived from the Italian *primaverola* (think "primavera"), that is, *fior di prima vera,* or "the first flower of spring." Under current nomenclatural law, the cowslip (*P. veris*) is considered the standard or type against which all other primulas are compared, hence the Latin species name *veris,* which means "true to type" or "standard."

The common English name of cowslip sounds lyrical enough at first, but in fact, its origins are considerably less refined. It's a polite form of the Saxon *cu-sloppe* or *cu-slyppe* — although most of us would be more familiar with the term "cow pie." The name must have arisen from the idea that since cowslips thrive in rich soils, they tended to grow in areas where cattle had recently been seen lifting their tails.

The cowslip is likely the most widely distributed of all primulas, its natural range stretching over 9,000 kilometres from Ireland and Norway east to Siberia, ending just short of the Pacific coast in China. Preferring a sunny situation with moist, humus-rich soil, the cowslip is hardy from Zones 3 to 8. Growing to a height of about 25 cm (10 inches),

One of the easiest primulas to propagate and once a common Eurasian wildflower (from Ireland to China), in its natural environment the cowslip (Primula veris) fell prey to modern tillage techniques and the increased use of agricultural herbicides after World War II. It is pictured here with the emerging fronds of Japanese painted fern (Athyrium niponicum var. pictum).

cowslips produce nodding umbels (flower clusters) of fragrant, deep yellow flowers up to 2 cm (¾ inch) across.

Cowslips are easy and inexpensive to propagate — they're one of the first perennials I ever grew from seed. I prefer to sow *Primula* seeds indoors in late winter, so that I can keep an eye on them, although in the Pacific Northwest they can be successfully sown directly in the garden. Cowslip seeds are widely available, but make sure you get a package with a "Best Before" date on it, since old stock will not germinate well. Transplants may be moved outdoors after all danger of frost is past, but before the soil gets too hot.

Plants grown from seed will take one to two years to flower, but after that, you can look forward to cowslips forever and ever. Given the moisture they crave, plants self-seed easily but not invasively. In areas where summers are extremely hot, it pays to grow cowslips in partly shaded conditions. Nevertheless, if the heat becomes too hellish, cowslips simply pack up their leaves and hide underground until the return of the autumn rains, although they will be less likely to self-seed under these conditions.

Intensive soil tillage and the expanded use of herbicides after World War II came close to decimating the natural populations of this wildflower, which once had been common across most of Britain. Cowslips were also subject to many centuries of intensive picking and marauding since they were widely used in traditional herbal medicine, as well as for decoration. Fortunately with the passing of new government legislation in 1975 restricting the picking of wildflowers (coupled with the backlash against the indiscriminate use of agricultural chemicals), the cowslip has begun to make a comeback in the land that first made it famous and then proceeded to almost exterminate it.

One of the best known and most cherished of all European plants, cowslips are frequently referred to in Shakespeare's plays. Comparing the flowers to Queen Elizabeth I's pensioners he wrote in *A Midsummer Night's Dream:*

The cowslips tall her pensioners be;
In their gold coats spots you see;
Those be rubies, fairy favours;
In those freckles live their savours.
    (Act II, Sc. i)

The ruby spots that Shakespeare alludes to are "floral markers" that help to guide pollinators to the nectaries. Shakespeare also seemed to be aware that the insects that are primarily responsible for fertilizing cowslips (unlike *Primula vulgaris*) are bees, and he transformed this simple fact of nature into Puck's famous song in *The Tempest:*

Where the bee sucks, there suck I
In a cowslip's bell I lie;
And there do crouch when owls do cry.
    (Act V, Sc. i)

the primrose

Primula vulgaris is a name that puts some gardeners off, but at the time these specific epithets (species names) were being handed out, "vulgar" didn't mean "rude" — it simply meant common, which *P. vulgaris* certainly is, in the best possible sense of the word. Native to most of Europe, the common primrose is also found growing wild from Gibraltar to Tunisia, one of only two species of *Primula* indigenous to the African continent.

With a history as long and as august as the cowslip, the common primrose without a doubt elicits a similar devotion among gardeners. Preferring the same moist, humus-rich soils as the cowslip, the primrose is hardy from Zones 4 to 8. In warmer zones, primroses require partly shaded conditions and will thrive best in cool areas — especially north-facing sites — while in cooler zones, they will favour a sunnier aspect.

Blooming in early to mid-spring, common primroses produce clusters of superb pale yellow blooms, each one up to 4 cm (1 ½ inches) across. Almost as easy to grow from fresh seed as the cowslip, seeds should be started indoors in late winter so that transplants will be ready to move outside by late spring. Once established in the damp garden, *Primula vulgaris* may be depended upon to self-seed modestly each year, although if you have some industrious ants nearby, you can look forward to better than average results.

Like our native bloodroot (*Sanguinaria canadensis*), and unlike any of its relatives, common primrose seeds are endowed with a gelatinous outgrowth (or elaiosome) that ants find irresistible. Consequently, the foraging ants return home with their bounty of sumptuous seeds, explaining at once why primroses are frequently found clustered around old ant nests.

The common primrose didn't escape Charles Darwin's eagle eye either. He was one of the first scientists to document the unorthodox arrangement of the reproductive parts of *Primula vulgaris*. He quickly noticed that within this single species, two very different types of stamens (the male flower parts that produce pollen) and stigmas (female flower parts where pollen is deposited) were being generated simultaneously. In one type (called "pin-eyed") a long, prominent stigma was produced while the stamens remained buried deep within the flower, and in the other type ("thrum-eyed") a very short stigma was produced alongside prominent, protruding stamens. Without getting too technical, this arrangement guaranteed cross-fertilization between different flower types, while prohibiting self-fertilization within a single flower, in the end ensuring an even shuffling of genes between plants.

The common primrose has given rise to many floral mutants over the centuries. Elizabethan gardeners adored types with double flowers, as well as semi-doubles, which were known as "Hose-in-hose" or "Jack in the green." Colour breaks with silver or gold-edged petals were also popular, and have enjoyed a further renaissance at the beginning of the twenty-first century (e.g., *Primula* 'Gold Lace'). *Primula vulgaris* is also a parent plant to most of the modern strains and cultivars that adorn nursery benches in late winter, including the gaudy multicolours of our popular 'Pacific Giant' series. As useful as these new cultivars are to modern gardeners, I think it would be impossible to improve on the original species type, which has inspired so many poets over the years:

Aske me why I send you here
This sweet Infanta of the yeere?

Ask me why I send to you
This Primrose, thus bepearl'd with dew?
    –The Primrose *by Robert Herrick*
    (1591–1674)

shooting star

(dodecatheon meadia)

It would be remiss of me to leave the Primulaceae family without mentioning our native *Dodecatheon* genus. Commonly known as shooting star or American cowslip, these plants are properly spring ephemerals like Virginia bluebells (*Mertensia pulmonarioides*) and purple corydalis (*Corydalis solida*). The hardiest and most widely distributed of the shooting stars is *Dodecatheon meadia*, which enjoys the same moist, humusy soil that cowslips and primroses relish. Hardy from Zones 4 to 8, it produces umbels of 2 cm (¾ inch) long magenta flowers before disappearing completely until the following spring, a situation that makes plant tags indispensable.

Gardeners in the Pacific Northwest are spoiled for choice when it comes to shooting stars and should watch for the following species at their local garden centres, all of which are hardy from Zones 5 to 7:

BOTANICAL NAME	COMMON NAME	ORIGIN
D. clevelandii	none	California
D. dentatum	none	W. North America
D. hendersonii	Mosquito bills, Sailor caps	California
D. pulchellum	syn. *D. pauciflorum*	W. North America

Always the exhibitionist, I like to combine the magenta flowers of our native shooting star (Dodecatheon meadia) *with the striking foliage of* Iris pallida *'Variegata'. It's important to remember that even naturalized gardens should bear the artistic stamp of their owners.*

NAME:

Gooseneck loosestrife
(*Lysimachia clethroides*)

HEIGHT:

90 cm (3 feet)

HARDY TO:

Zone 3

EXPOSURE:

Full sun

BLOOMING PERIOD:

Mid to late summer

SOIL:

Requires a moist soil of
average fertility

COMPANIONS:

Lovely in a large swath by
itself, or combined with
flowering shrubs

SPECIAL NOTES:

Gooseneck loosestrife
makes a gorgeous cut
flower, and it's prolific
enough that you needn't
worry about denuding
the garden.

gooseneck loosestrife

lysimachia clethroides

The genus *Lysimachia* contains about 150 species, but is (somewhat surprisingly) a member of the much larger Primrose (Primulaceae) family. Most gardeners recoil in horror when they hear the name loosestrife uttered, imagining expanses of purple flowers choking local waterways unchecked, but rest assured, gooseneck loosestrife is an altogether different plant and completely unrelated to the pestilential purple loosestrife (*Lythrum salicaria*).

Several European species of *Lysimachia* have been used for millennia in herbal medicine, and it would appear that this is how the common name loosestrife evolved. Writing in the first century A.D., the Roman physician Pliny (23–79) asserted that it was useful for soothing angry animals, and that if a pair of oxen quarrelled, a spray of the plant laid across their shoulders would immediately pacify them or "loose them from their strife."

Several other *Lysimachia* species also bear the common name loosestrife, notably *L. punctata* (whorled loosestrife) and *L. vulgaris* (yellow loosestrife). The genus is named after Lysimachus (306–281 BCE), King of Thrace (part of present-day Greece, Bulgaria, and Turkey), while the species name *clethroides* means "with flowers like *Clethra*."

Native to China, Korea, and Japan, gooseneck loosestrife produces many small, saucer-shaped white flowers (up to 1.5 cm / ½ inch across) in arching clusters from mid to late summer. Hardy from Zones 3 to 9, gooseneck loosestrife isn't fussy about the soil that anchors it, but it does require a full sun location and consistent moisture throughout the growing season if it is to be seen at its best.

The curving, pendant clusters of flowers that gooseneck loosestrife produces are always eye-catching, and I consider that when it's in bloom, it's one of the finest architectural plants in the garden. As the flowers begin to mature, they assume a more upright stance, so that the effect becomes stiffer and slightly more formal, and although gooseneck loosestrife grows as tall as 90 cm (3 feet), it never needs staking unless it is grown in dry soil.

Most of the lysimachias have a reputation for spreading quickly and vigorously, and *L. clethroides* is no exception. Seldom setting much seed (making autumn deadheading an optional chore), gooseneck loosestrife instead spreads by means of robust underground roots that are capable of popping up a considerable distance away from the parent plant. While this sort of behaviour might not be considered appropriate for a controlled, manicured herbaceous border, it's just the sort of thing we're after in the

Absolutely unrelated to the
dreaded purple loosestrife
(Lythrum salicaria),
gooseneck loosestrife
(Lysimachia clethroides)
belongs to an entirely separate
plant family (Primulaceae).
As it's one of the finest
architectural plants in the
naturalized garden, and
a flower arranger's dream-
come-true, it's small wonder
that Abigail Moreland keeps
such a proprietary eye on her
splendid plot.

naturalized garden. Some degree of control may be exercised over gooseneck loosestrife if it is planted among other equally assertive plants such as meadow cranesbill (*Geranium pratense* and cvs.), goldenrod (*Solidago* cvs.), golden groundsel (*Ligularia spp.* and cvs.), or deeply rooted shrubs.

Several of our native Lysimachias are also suitable for inclusion in the naturalized damp garden. *Lysimachia ciliata* is not a very prepossessing plant in and of itself, but

I usually recommend that gardeners commence their introduction to lysimachias with *L. clethroides*, but there's no need to stop there. Providing you can supply sufficient space, there are plenty more *Lysimachia* hopefuls waiting in the wings:

BOTANICAL NAME	COMMON NAME	ORIGIN	COLOUR	ZONES
L. barystachys	none	Asia	White	4 to 9
L. congestiflora	Dense-flowered loosestrife	China	Yellow	6 to 9
L. ephemerum	none	Spain	White	7 to 9
L. longifolia	none	N. America	Yellow	4 to 8
L. japonica 'Minutissima'	none	Eurasia	Yellow	6 to 9
L. nummularia 'Aurea'	Golden creeping Jenny	Eurasia	Yellow	4 to 8
L. punctata	Whorled loosestrife	Europe	Yellow	4 to 8
L. vulgaris	Yellow loosestrife	Eurasia	Yellow	5 to 9

the purple-leaved form (*L. ciliata* 'Purpurea') is a striking individual, growing between 60 and 80 cm (2 and 2 ½ feet) tall and hardy from Zones 3 to 9. Bearing star-shaped yellow flowers (2.5 cm / 1 inch across) in mid-summer, the real attraction here is the foliage, which, when new, looks almost black.

Although gooseneck loosestrife wasn't introduced to Western gardens until 1869, William Robinson had already made its acquaintance when he wrote of it: "a graceful plant with long nodding dense spikes of white blossoms, and the leaves in autumn of brilliant hues."

Margery Fish appears to have been equally smitten: "It is quite an effective plant, especially if it can be planted with its back to a wall or hedge. Then all the graceful flowers point the same way, whereas if grown in an open bed they don't really know which way to look. The leaves of this *Lysimachia* turn crimson in autumn and it associates well with the herbaceous *Clematis heracleifolia* var. *davidiana*."

While I think that in our climate, gooseneck loosestrife would almost certainly overwhelm any herbaceous *Clematis*, it still evokes a lovely visual — the tubular light blue, scented flowers of the *Clematis*, scrambling up through those graceful goosenecks!

MORE PERENNIALS FOR THE NATURALIZED DAMP GARDEN

In addition to the plants that we've examined in detail, there are many more which warrant a place in the naturalized damp garden. Here are thirty more suggestions to get you going:

NAME	ORIGIN	ZONES
Astilbe (*Astilbe* cvs.)	Asia, N. America	4 to 9
Black snakeroot (*Cimicifuga spp.*)	Asia, N. America	4 to 8
Bleeding heart (*Dicentra spp.* and cvs.)	Asia, N. America	3 to 8
Bugleweed (*Ajuga reptans* and cvs.)	Europe, Iran	3 to 9
Celandine poppy (*Stylophorum diphyllum*)	N. America	5 to 9
Darmera peltata (syn. *Peltiphyllum*)	N. America	5 to 9
Daylily (*Hemerocallis spp.* and cvs.)	Asia	3 to 10
Elephant's ears (*Bergenia spp.* and cvs.)	Asia	4 to 8
Foam flower (*Tiarella cordifolia* and cvs.)	N. America	3 to 7
Globeflower (*Trollius spp.* and cvs.)	Eurasia, N. America	5 to 8
Goatsbeard (*Aruncus dioicus*)	Europe, N. America	3 to 7
Golden spurge (*Euphorbia palustris*)	Eurasia	5 to 8
Gunnera manicata	Colombia to Brazil	7 to 10
Knotweed (*Persicaria spp.* and cvs.)	Widely distributed	4 to 8
Lady's mantle (*Alchemilla mollis*)	Caucasus, Turkey	3 to 7
Lords and ladies (*Arum italicum* 'Marmoratum')	Europe, N. Africa	6 to 9
Meadow rue (*Thalictrum spp.* and cvs.)	Widely distributed	5 to 8
Milky bellflower (*Campanula lactiflora* and cvs.)	Caucasus, Turkey	5 to 7
Obedient plant (*Physostegia virginiana* and cvs.)	N. America	4 to 8
Plantain lily (*Hosta spp.* [most])	Asia	3 to 8
Purple avens (*Geum rivale* and cvs.)	Europe	3 to 8
Rheum palmatum 'Atrosanguineum'	China, Tibet	5 to 9
Rodgersia aesculifolia	China	5 to 8
Siberian bugloss (*Brunnera macrophylla*)	Caucasus	3 to 7
Siberian iris (*Iris sibirica* and cvs)	Europe	4 to 9
Snake's-head fritillary (*Fritillaria meleagris*)	Europe	3 to 8
Snowflake (*Leucojum spp.* and cvs.)	Europe	4 to 9
Spiderwort (*Tradescantia* Andersoniana Group)	N. America	4 to 9
Toad lily (*Tricyrtis spp.* and cvs.)	Japan, Taiwan	4 to 9
White mugwort (*Artemisia lactiflora*)	Western China	5 to 8

NAME:
Great blue lobelia
(*Lobelia siphilitica*)

HEIGHT:
60 to 120 cm (2 to 4 feet)

HARDY TO:
Zone 3

EXPOSURE:
Prefers part shade, will
tolerate full sun

BLOOMING PERIOD:
Late summer to mid-autumn

SOIL:
Prefers moist to wet soil
conditions, tolerant of dry
soils when grown in shade

COMPANIONS:
I like to grow my great blue
lobelia in conjunction with
other plants that bloom at
the same period. Although
these others are not natives,
I love it with grape-leaved
anemone (*Anemone
tomentosa* 'Superba')
and yellow wax-bells
(*Kirengeshoma palmata*).

SPECIAL NOTES:
Many of the newer *Lobelia* ×
speciosa cultivars look lovely
with the straight species
types. Especially worthy are
the 'Compliment' and 'Fan'
series, which in spite of
being perennial are often
sold as annuals in cell
packs. What a bargain!

great blue lobelia

lobelia siphilitica

I've been trying to remember when I first grew *Lobelia siphilitica*, since it feels as if I've always had it. My best guess is that I bought seed at a native flower seed swap in first or second year university, and if memory serves me, it was collected near Stony Lake — Catherine Parr Traill's old stomping grounds.

Mrs. Traill certainly saw great blue lobelia growing wild, and commented: "The largest and most showy, but not often cultivated, of the Lobelias, is *L. siphilitica*, a stout-stemmed, many-flowered species, which is chiefly found near springs; the flowers are full blue and the spike much crowded; the height about eighteen or twenty inches; leaves light green."

There is no doubt that the more water you can supply to great blue lobelia, the better it will grow, but like Joe Pye weed (*Eupatorium purpureum*) it will also grow in much drier conditions. I myself have a rather fine stand sharing a root zone and enduring the shade cast by my despised Norway maple (*Acer platanoides* 'Crimson King'), and I'm confident that if they can make it there, they can make it anywhere. Margery Fish worried that "the lovely blue siphilitica is often distressed after a long dry spell" but I have found that plants can withstand drought much more readily if they're grown in a shady location.

The *Lobelia* genus comprises about 370 species, most of them native to the Western hemisphere. Named for Mathias de l'Obel (1538–1616), King's Botanist to James I of England, the de l'Obel family had derived their name from the 'Abele' or white poplar tree (now *Populus albus*), so that the name has been transferred from plants to people, and then back again from people to plants.

Great blue lobelia was introduced to Europe around 1665, although at this time it was commonly known as blue cardinal flower, since the closely related *Lobelia cardinalis* (Cardinal flower) had been introduced some years prior. It was Carl Linnaeus (1707–78), father of modern botanical nomenclature, who finally assigned the species name *siphilitica*, or as one Victorian writer tersely wrote: "Linnaeus gave this plant its repellent specific name." Repellent or not, Linnaeus mounted this tribute to venereal disease with good reason: One of his pupils (Peter Kalm) had visited New England in 1747 and had become acquainted with the Iroquois custom of using a root decoction to treat and cure syphilis. Eventually Sir William Johnson (Superintendent of Indian Affairs in North America from 1756 to 1774) sent seeds of the plant back to English physicians hoping to furnish a cure, and although in the end the tonic proved ineffective, the risqué name stuck.

Although we now have more effective means of treating syphilis, Lobelia siphilitica is nevertheless an invaluable plant for the damp garden. Contrasting nicely with the irrepressible golden shades of autumn, the blue spires of great blue lobelia associate well with the pink blooms of grape-leaved anemone (Anemone tomentosa 'Superba') and the pale yellow shuttlecocks of yellow wax-bells (Kirengeshoma palmata).

Lobelia siphilitica must surely be one of the most carefree plants in the natural garden. It seems a waste to purchase plants at a nursery when they are so simple to grow from seed, preferring moist soil conditions on a partially shaded site. There is no need to start plants off indoors — scattering seed on the soil surface (remember to mark the area) out of doors in late autumn or early spring will do the trick admirably. Once the seedlings appear in mid-spring, they should be thinned out, leaving about 30 cm (1 foot) between plants. Most seedlings will form only a leafy rosette in their first year, although there will likely be some precocious individuals that will send up a tentative flowering spike in their first year.

Never space great blue lobelia too sparsely — it is a tall (80 cm / 32 inches or more) plant and needs to be planted fairly densely to achieve a good effect. Although it blooms slightly earlier than some of the blue autumn gentians (*Gentiana spp.*), it lasts for at least four or five weeks as the flowers gradually open from the bottom of the floral spike, eventually scaling its tip by mid to late autumn.

After their flowering has ceased, I generally try to deadhead plants since sufficient seed will already have been set to secure a new generation of plants. Curiously, plants that grow in ideal conditions (moist soil, part shade) seem to be much shorter lived than those grown in less hospitable situations, so a few new plants are always welcome.

The other reason that I would encourage you to take the "seeding approach" to propagation is that you are much more likely to get some genetic variation when you grow plants from seed. The first year my plants bloomed, I was amazed to find that along with the blue forms, there were also several white-flowered plants (sometimes classified as *Lobelia siphilitica* f. *albiflora*), but even more exciting, by the second year, I had plants that produced bi-coloured blue flowers streaked with white, and white flowers streaked with blue. These bi-coloured natural crosses tend to be shorter, squatter plants, but they are quite exquisite in their intricacies.

Lobelia cardinalis (Cardinal flower) is often mentioned in the same breath as *L. siphilitica,* and in its native environment it will grow just as magnificently. Unfortunately, cardinal flower appears to be much more particular about its siting, and I have yet to get more than two seasons out of a single plant. I admit this only because I know I'm not alone, and even Graham Stuart Thomas characterizes Cardinal flower as "unreliable."

In the never-ending quest to develop showier, hardier ornamentals for the garden, many crosses between *Lobelia cardinalis* and *L. siphilitica* have been made, commencing as early as 1777. The most successful of these crosses were created by W. M. Bowden in Ontario during the 1960s and 70s, and these trial plants were promptly shipped to the Royal Horticultural Society gardens at Wisley in Surrey, where they quickly earned many plaudits.

Some of the most successful crosses between great blue lobelia and Cardinal flower occurred in Ontario and now make up a large share of the hardy *Lobelia* market. Almost as hardy as *Lobelia siphilitica,* they look much more like *L. cardinalis,* enabling you to add some red tones to the mix. Keep an eye out for the following cultivars, now known collectively as 'Bowden Hybrids':

CULTIVAR NAME	COLOUR	HEIGHT	ZONES
'Brightness'	Blood red	90 cm (3 feet)	4 to 9
'Cherry Ripe'	Cherry red	90 cm (3 feet)	3 to 8
'Dark Crusader'	Deep red	75 cm (30 inches)	4 to 8
'Will Scarlet'	Bright red	90 cm (3 feet)	4 to 8

joe pye weed

eupatorium purpureum

The genus *Eupatorium* was once vast (with over 1,000 species), but botanists have recently moved at least half of these into other genera such as *Ageratina* and *Bartlettina*. Never mind, the very best eupatoriums are native to North America, and generally hardy to Zone 3. Used for centuries in herbal medicine, the genus is named for the Persian king of Pontus, Mithridates Eupator (120–63 BCE), who won several important battles against the Romans, and who apparently used a species of *Eupatorium* as an antidote to poison.

The common name of Joe Pye weed is applied not just to *Eupatorium purpureum*, but also to the closely related *E. fistulosum* and *E. maculatum*, all three of which are native to much of the North American landmass. Whether or not someone named "Joe Pye" ever actually existed is open to discussion since he has been variously reported as "a 19th-century Caucasian" as well as "an Indian medicine man who lived in Colonial New England." All accounts agree, however, that Joe Pye became famous for concocting *Eupatorium*-based "simples" (or herbal remedies) that cured typhoid fever. Certainly the plant must have had some connection with typhoid since *jopi* is the word used for "typhoid fever" in several Amerindian dialects and could easily have been corrupted over the years as "Joe Pye." Interestingly, recent German research has found that many *Eupatorium spp.* contain immunologically active polysaccharides, and further investigation is ongoing.

Catherine Parr Traill knew the hardy eupatoriums (including *E. perfoliatum* or boneset) as thorough-wort or trumpet weed and gives a fascinating account regarding their use by "the old Canadian and Yankee settlers" (United Empire Loyalists): "In case of accidents, such as wounds from axes, broken limbs, and such ailments as agues and fevers, necessity compelled active measures to be adopted on the spot; medical-practitioners, so called, there were none; the broken limbs were set by those in the settlement possessed of the most nerve, while the elder women bound up the wounds, or gathered the healing herbs which they had learned to distinguish by experience, or from oral tradition, as being curative in certain disorders. Something of this healing art was derived from their ancestors, who had the knowledge from the Indian medicine-men."

Herbal history aside, *Eupatorium purpureum* is one of the showiest of all native plants, and no natural garden should be considered complete without it. Bearing panicles (branching clusters) of deep purple-pink flowers from late summer to autumn, the leaves of Joe Pye weed are arranged in circular whorls, similar to those of sweet woodruff (*Galium*

NAME:
Joe Pye weed
(*Eupatorium purpureum*)
HEIGHT:
2 m (7 feet)
HARDY TO:
Zone 3
EXPOSURE:
Prefers full sun, tolerates partial shade
BLOOMING PERIOD:
Late summer to mid-autumn
SOIL:
Average soil, thrives in damp conditions
COMPANIONS:
I grow my Joe Pye weed with the related European species, *Eupatorium cannabinum* 'Plenum' (a sterile, double-flowered hybrid). Also lovely with Culver's root (*Veronicastrum virginicum*) and zebra grass (*Miscanthus sinensis* 'Zebrinus')
SPECIAL NOTES:
For a really outstanding display, attempt to group several species of *Eupatorium* together. They'll leave you gasping!

Joe Pye weed (Eupatorium purpureum) (background) and hemp agrimony (E. cannabinum) (foreground) are both plants that require plenty of elbow room. Spreading primarily by underground runners, they produce magnificent purple stems that last long after the late-season flowers have faded. No one's really sure if Joe Pye ever actually existed, but his namesakes will all add colour, height, and texture to the naturalized damp garden.

odoratum) although on a much larger scale. But like Margery Fish, it is the purple stems of Joe Pye weed that I admire for much of the season: "*Eupatorium purpureum* grows 6 – 8' and more, and makes a splendid thicket of dark stems, after its flat purple flowers."

The flowers of Joe Pye weed are a story in themselves. Although the size of the flowering panicles are large and imposing (15 to 20 cm / 6 to 8 inches across), they are in fact made up of many hundreds of disc-like florets, botanically similar in form and function to the central yellow eye of the common daisy. It is the distribution of these florets that compose the actual flower, but Joe Pye weed differs from the daisy in that it doesn't actually possess a single petal and is instead made up of many bisexual (or "perfect") florets, containing both pistils and stamens within a single structure.

Joe Pye weed will reach its fullest floral potential when grown in damp conditions, although it will certainly perform satisfactorily in drier arenas. The easiest way to commence your acquaintance with Joe Pye weed is to purchase a few plants at your local nursery, and with luck, they will have several species available so that you can initiate a fledgling *Eupatorium* collection straight away. Be vigilant when it comes to spacing new plants, since most Joe Pye weed varieties need plenty of elbow room, and usually attain a girth of at least 1 m (3 feet) at maturity. Like most plants that enjoy a slightly soggy environment, Joe Pye weed will reward you in the end if you get it off to a good start with lots of organic matter and perhaps a handful or two of bone meal. Many texts will tell you that Joe Pye weed prefers a slightly alkaline soil, but it will also grow quite acceptably in moderately acidic conditions.

By mid-autumn *Eupatorium purpureum* will have produced plenty of seed (although the "flower heads" are still ornamental), but it could never be considered an abundant self-seeder. Like so many of our native plants, it spreads much more rapidly and efficiently by sending out underground roots, which produce new plants in an ever widening circle. If clumps become too overwhelming, peripheral plants may be dug up and replanted in other parts of the garden, or better still, passed on to gardening cohorts.

Joe Pye weed is naturally a tall, statuesque plant, and I like to leave it that way. However, gardeners dealing with smaller spaces may find it necessary to control the height of the plant, which is easily achieved by cutting plants back in mid-June. When it's cut back to just above a whorl of leaves, five new shoots will appear. In the end, you'll have a shorter, multi-branched plant with slightly smaller panicles. Plants treated in this way

Culver's root (Veronicastrum virginicum, *pictured here*) is native from Ontario to Texas and hardy to Zone 3. Enjoying the same moist, sunny conditions as Joe Pye weed (Eupatorium purpureum), *Culver's root grows to a height of 2 m (6 feet) and is therefore capable of holding its own in the Land of the Giants!*

may also be shaped to encourage a more mounded, rounded form, using the same method as with willow blue star (*Amsonia tabernaemontana*) — simply cut back peripheral stems by half, gradually decreasing the cut until you get to the centre of the plant, which you can leave untouched.

Although *Eupatorium purpureum* is likely the best plant for noviciates to begin with, there are several other *Eupatorium spp.* that deserve a place in the naturalized damp garden:

NAME	AVAILABLE CULTIVARS	ZONES
Boneset (*E. perfoliatum*)	none	3 to 9
Hardy ageratum (*E. coelestinum*)	'Cori', 'Wayside'	3 to 7
Hemp agrimony (Europe) (*E. cannabinum*)	'Plenum'	3 to 9
Joe Pye weed (*E. fistulosum*)	'Gateway', 'Selection'	3 to 8
Joe Pye weed (*E. maculatum*)	'Atropurpureum'	3 to 7
White snakeroot (*E. rugosum*)	'Chocolate'	4 to 9

NAME:

Virginia bluebells
(*Mertensia pulmonarioides*)

HEIGHT:

30 to 45 cm (12 to 18 inches)

HARDY TO:

Zone 3

EXPOSURE:

Part shade to full sun

BLOOMING PERIOD:

Mid to late spring

SOIL:

Prefers a rich soil with
ample moisture during
active growth

COMPANIONS:

Great with primroses
(*Primula spp.* and cvs.),
bleeding heart (*Dicentra spp.*
and cvs.), and ferns, but
probably at its best when
performing solo

SPECIAL NOTES:

Gardeners in the Pacific
Northwest should experi-
ment with local species of
Mertensia such as M. *ciliata*
(mountain bluebell) while
East Coast gardeners will
likely achieve better results
with M. *maritima* (oyster
plant).

virginia bluebells

mertensia pulmonarioides

Formerly known as *Mertensia virginica* (a much easier name for most gardeners to pro-nounce), *M. pulmonarioides* is the most ornamental of the fifty or so species of *Mertensia*, about half of which are native to North America. Named for the German botanist Franz Karl Mertens (1764–1831), the specific name refers to the resemblance between Virginia bluebells and members of the *Pulmonaria* (Lungwort) genus, both of which belong to the much larger Borage (Boraginaceae) family.

Like purple coneflower (*Echinacea purpurea*), the seeds of Virginia bluebells were sent from Virginia to the Oxford Botanic Garden by the ill-fated John Banister and even-tually they became fairly widely grown in both England and Germany. The great garden designer Gertrude Jekyll called them "the very embodiment of the freshness of early spring." She had likely been influenced in this opinion by her mentor, William Robinson, who felt that the "Virginian cowslip" as he called it, was "the handsomest of the Mertensias, bearing in early spring drooping clusters of lovely purple-blue blossoms. It is an old garden plant, and one which has never become common; in the southern country it is grown too dry."

It is true that Virginia bluebells require plenty of water while they are in active growth from early spring to early summer, but quite frankly, after that it really doesn't matter whether they receive any moisture or not. This is because, like purple corydalis (*Corydalis solida*), they are technically spring ephemerals, and once they have bloomed, set seed, and their foliage has matured, all above-ground evidence of their existence disappears completely.

Blooming from mid to late spring and hardy from Zones 3 to 7, Virginia bluebells are native from western New York and southern Ontario, west to Arkansas and Kansas and as far north as Minnesota and Manitoba. Needless to say, any species that can thrive in such diverse conditions is a prime candidate for inclusion in the naturalized garden.

Requiring plenty of moisture while in active growth (early spring to early summer), like all spring ephemerals Virginia bluebells (Mertensia pulmonarioides) will batten down the hatches at the first sign of serious summer heat. To ensure a generous display, allow seed heads to mature once flowering has ceased.

In addition to *Mertensia pulmonarioides*, there are several other species which will prove useful in the naturalized garden:

NAME	ORIGIN	ZONES
M. sibirica (syn. *M. pterocarpa*)	Siberia, E. Asia	3 to 7
M. simplicissima (syn. *M. asiatica*)	Russia, Korea, Japan	6 to 8
Mountain bluebell (*M. ciliata*)	Rocky Mountains	4 to 7
Himalayan bluebell (*M. echioides*)	Himalayas	6 to 9
Oyster plant (*M. maritima*)	N. America, N. Europe	3 to 7
Tall lungwort (*M. paniculata*)	N. Ontario, Midwest USA	3 to 7

One of the earliest plants to show in the springtime, *Mertensia pulmonarioides* grows to a height of between 30 and 45 cm (12 to 18 inches) and bears cymes (branching clusters) of pink buds that open into tubular sky-blue or purple-blue flowers up to 2.5 cm (1 inch) long. A white form is sometimes available and sold under the name 'Alba', as well as a pink form called 'Rubra', but to my eye, the blue varieties are the most enchanting.

Because Virginia bluebells require extra moisture while they are in active growth, they are best sited in a damp section of the garden where they can be grown in part to full sun. In drier conditions (under deciduous trees, for example), they will likely require a partly shaded area in order to prosper. I have seen magnificent clumps of Virginia bluebells growing at the base of large trees in the Toronto area and have also observed equally glorious drifts growing in open exposed surroundings farther north, so it would appear that plants grown in cooler zones will appreciate some extra sunlight.

If you intend to buy fully grown plants (likely the most expedient way to get started), they should be purchased in early spring and installed immediately. Never deadhead Virginia bluebells, since the whole idea is to let them carpet an area, and they will do this in just a few years if seed is allowed to ripen on the plant and drop naturally. If you're lucky enough to find a retail seed source for Virginia bluebells, by all means take advantage of it since they are easy to propagate by spreading seed on the soil surface in late spring and then keeping the area consistently moist for the first season. Grown this way, they will take three years to flower. A third method frequently used to increase stock is to divide the brittle roots immediately after the foliage has died down, or alternatively in the early autumn — the point being to carry out the procedure when plants are dormant, while at the same time avoiding the intense heat of midsummer.

In addition to ample moisture, Virginia bluebells require soil with a fairly high percentage of organic matter, so you'll want to prepare the planting area with compost, shredded leaves, and/or composted manure. Many gardeners feel that like daffodils (*Narcissus spp.* and cvs.), the blue-green foliage of Virginia bluebells tends to outstay its welcome, and it's irrefutable that it turns a hideous yellow-tan shade just before disappearing. The trick is to camouflage the maturing foliage by installing other plants beside it that wake up slightly later in the season, such as *Astilbe* cultivars, ferns, and hardy geraniums (*Geranium spp.* and cvs.).

Be sure to include Virginia bluebells in your damp garden — you'll be thankful that you did next spring!

appendix

plant & catalogue source list

Canada

AIMERS
126 Catherine Street North
Hamilton, ON L8R 1J4
Phone: 905-529-2601
Fax: 905-528-1635
E-mail: **aimers.seed@sympatico.ca**

A wide selection of wildflower seeds

BLUESTEM ORNAMENTAL GRASSES
1949 Fife Road
Christina Lake, BC V0H 1E3
Phone & Fax: 250-447-6363

Ornamental grasses and plugs of native
and exotic species

BOUGHEN NURSERIES
P.O. Box 12
Valley River, MB R0L 2B0
Phone: 204-638-7618
Fax: 204-638-7172

Specializing in plants and shrubs for
gardeners in Zones 1 to 3

CORN HILL NURSERIES
2700 Route 890
Corn Hill, NB E4Z 1M2
Phone: 506-756-3635
Fax: 506-756-1087

Hardy flowering shrubs, vines, and roses

CRUICKSHANK'S AT INDIGO
780 Birchmount Road, Unit 16
Scarborough, ON M1K 5H4
Phone: 800-665-5605
Fax: 416-750-8522
www.cruickshanks.com

Specializing in bulbous plants, many
suitable for naturalizing

WILLIAM DAM SEEDS
P.O. Box 8400
Dundas, ON L9H 6M1
Phone: 905-628-6641
Fax: 905-627-1729
www.damseeds.com

Specializing in untreated seeds

DOMINION SEED HOUSE
P.O. Box 2500
Georgetown, ON L7G 5L6
Phone: 800-784-3037
Fax: 800-282-5746
www.dominion-seed-house.com

Large selection of plants, flower and
vegetable seeds, and bulbs

FLORABUNDA SEEDS
P.O. Box 3
Indian River, ON K0L 2B0
www.florabundaseeds.com

Wildflower, heirloom, and medicinal
herb seeds

FRAGRANT FLORA
R.R. 22
3741 Sunshine Coast Highway
Roberts Creek, BC V0N 2W2
Phone & Fax: 604-885 6142
E-mail: **fragrantflora@sunshine.net**

Fragrant plants with an emphasis on
species that attract hummingbirds
and butterflies

FRASER'S THIMBLE FARMS
175 Arbutus Road
Salt Spring Island, BC V8K 1A3
Phone & Fax: 250-537-5788
www.thimblefarms.com

Specializing in *Corydalis, Erythronium,*
ferns, hardy orchids, and *Trillium*

GARDENS NORTH
5984 3rd Line Road North
North Gower, ON K0A 2T0
Phone: 613-489-0065
Fax: 613-489-1208
www.gardensnorth.com

Seeds for rare perennials and woody species,
both native and introduced

HUMBER NURSERIES
R.R. 8
Brampton, ON L6T 3Y7
Phone: 416-798-8733
Fax: 905-794-1311
www.humbernurseries.on.ca

Comprehensive listings in all plant categories

NATURAL INSECT CONTROL
R.R. 2
Stevensville, ON L0S 1S0
Phone: 905-382-2904
Fax: 905-382-4418
www.natural-insect-control.com

Beneficial insects by mail

OSC SEEDS

P.O. Box 7
330 Phillip St
Waterloo, ON N2J 3Z6
Phone: 519-886-0557
Fax: 519-886-0605
www.oscseeds.com

Untreated wildflower, herb, native grass, and wetland seeds

PICKERING NURSERIES

670 Kingston Road
Pickering, ON L1V 1A6
Phone: 905-839-2111
www.pickeringnurseries.com

A huge selection including hardy shrub roses and Agriculture Canada introductions

PRAIRIE HABITATS

P.O. Box 1
Argyle, MB R0C 0B0
Phone: 204-467-9371
www.prairiehabitats.com

Native wildflower and grass seed

RICHTERS HERBS

357 Highway 47
Goodwood, ON L0C 1A0
Phone: 905-640-6677
Fax: 905-640-6641
www.richters.com

A comprehensive listing of herbs and wildflowers, both native and introduced

SEEDS OF DISTINCTION

P.O. Box 86, Station 'A'
Toronto, ON M9C 4V2
Phone: 416-255-3060
Fax: 888-327-9193
www.seedsofdistinction.com

First-class selection of rare and unusual flower seeds

SEEDS OF DIVERSITY CANADA

P.O. Box 36, Station 'Q'
Toronto, ON M4T 2L7
Phone: 905-623-0353
www.seeds.ca

Seed exchange for rare, non-hybridized plants

SPILLNER'S SEEDHOUSE
P.O. Box 22035
Halifax, NS B3L 4T7
Phone: 902-477-3017
Fax: 902-477-3003
www.spillnersseedhouse.com

Specializing in seeds for shrubs and trees,
many native

STOKES SEEDS
P.O. Box 10, 39 James Street
St Catherines, ON L2R 6R6
Phone: 905-688-4300
Fax: 888-834-3334
www.stokeseeds.com

A large selection of flower, herb, and
vegetable seeds

VESEY'S SEEDS
P.O. Box 9000
Charlottetown, PE C1A 8K6
Phone: 800-363-7333
Fax: 902-566-1620
www.veseys.com

Specializing in plants for short
growing seasons

WILDFLOWER FARM
R.R. 3
Schomberg, ON L0G 1T0
www.wildflowerfarm.com

Online catalogue only, specializing
in native species

United States

HEIRLOOM SEEDS
P.O. Box 245
W. Elizabeth, PA 15088-0245
www.heirloomseeds.com

Open pollinated flower and vegetable seeds

HERONSWOOD NURSERY
7530 NE 288th Street
Kingston, WA 98346-9502
Phone: 360-297-4172
Fax: 360-297-8321
www.heronswood.com

With over 2600 listings, this is a catalogue
to be reckoned with

JOHNNY'S SELECTED SEEDS
1 Foss Hill Road
Albion, MA 04910-9731
Phone: 207-437-4301
Fax: 207-437-2165
www.johnnyseeds.com

A comprehensive listing

PARK SEED
1 Parkton Avenue
Greenwood, SC 29647-0001
Phone: 800-845-3369
Fax: 864-941-4206
www.parkseed.com

A venerable publication, first published in 1868

SELECT SEEDS ANTIQUE FLOWERS
180 Stickney Hill Road
Union, CT 06076-4617
Phone: 860-684-9310
Fax: 800-653-3304
www.selectseeds.com

An excellent source for old-fashioned
varieties

THOMPSON & MORGAN
P.O. Box 1308, Dept. 11
Jackson, NJ 08527
Phone: 800-274-7333
Fax: 888-466-4769
www.thompson-morgan.com

An inexhaustible listings of flowers, both
native and introduced

United Kingdom

CHILTERN SEEDS
Bortree Style
Ulverston, Cumbria
England LA12 7PB
Phone: 011-44-1229/581-137
Fax: 011-44-1229/584-549
www.chilternseeds.co.uk

Likely the largest, most encyclopaedic seed
catalogue in print

glossary

beneficial insect
Any insect that improves the soil, pollinates plants, or controls harmful pests.

binomial
The two words (usually in Latin) that make up the botanical or scientific names of plants. The first word identifies the genus, the second the species.

bisexual
In botany, having both stamens and pistils in the same flower. Such flowers are also called "perfect."

bonemeal
A high phosphorous fertilizer made from powdered animal bones.

calyx
Collectively, the sepals of a flower.

compost
Decomposed organic matter.

corolla
Collectively, the petals of a flower.

corymb
A flat-topped cluster of flowers that begin blooming at the edge and proceed toward the centre.

cross-pollination
The transfer of pollen from a flower on one plant to a flower on a different plant.

cultivar
A plant variety maintained in cultivation by vegetative propagation or from inbred seed. The word "cultivar" is derived from "*culti*vated *vari*ety."

cyme
A branched flower cluster that blooms from the centre toward the edges.

deadheading
Removing spent flowers during the growing season to encourage the development of new flowers and to prevent seed formation.

dioecious
Having male and female flowers on separate plants. Most hollies, junipers, and yews are dioecious.

division
The propagation of a plant by separating it into two or more pieces, each of which has at least one growth bud and some roots.

ecosystem
A community of plants, animals, and their environment, functioning as a unit.

exotic
A plant that is native to another part of the world but has been introduced here.

genus (plural: genera)
A group of plant species with similarities in flower form, and often in general appearance, growth habit, and cultural requirements. A single genus may include from one to over a thousand species. The name of the genus is the first word in the two-part Latin plant name.

humus
Organic matter derived from partially decomposed plant and animal remains.

leaf mould
Partially decayed or composted leaves.

microclimate
Local conditions of shade, exposure, wind, drainage, and other factors that affect plant growth at any particular site.

mutant
An accidental variation in a plant, such as the formation of variegated leaves or double flowers.

native
A plant that grows naturally in a particular region and was not introduced from another area.

N-P-K

The chemical symbols of the three major plant nutrients in a complete fertilizer: nitrogen (N), phosphorous (P), and potassium (K).

open-pollinated

A term used to describe varieties resulting from natural or uncontrolled pollination, as opposed to hybrids whose pollination is controlled.

organic matter

Plant and animal residues such as leaves, trimmings, and manure in various stages of decomposition.

panicle

A loose, branching cluster of flowers that bloom from the centre or bottom toward the edges or top.

perianth

Collectively, all the sepals and petals of a flower.

pistil

The complete female organ of reproduction in flowers.

rhizome

A horizontal underground stem, often swollen into a storage organ. Both roots and shoots emerge from rhizomes.

runner

A slender shoot that grows along the ground, forming roots and a new plant at its tip end.

self-pollination

The transfer of pollen from one flower to the same or other flowers on the same plant.

sepal

One of the outermost flower parts, arranged in a ring outside the petals. Although often green and leaf-like, it is sometimes large and colourful.

species

A group of individual plants that share many characteristics and interbreed freely. The second word in Latin plant names indicates the species.

stamen
> The male reproduction organ of a flower.

stolon
> A stem that runs along the ground, forming roots and new plants at intervals along its length.

taproot
> A long, tapering root that has little or no side growth.

umbel
> A flower cluster in which the individual flower stalks emerge from the same point on the stem, like the ribs of an umbrella.

unisexual flower
> A flower bearing only stamens or pistils, but not both.

variegated
> A term used to describe leaves that are marked, striped, or blotched with some colour other than green (usually white or yellow).

whorl
> A group of three or more leaves that emerge from a single node.

hardiness zones

HARDINESS ZONES OF MAJOR CANADIAN CITIES

St. John's, NF	Zone 5	Thunder Bay, ON	Zone 2
Halifax, NS	Zone 6	Winnipeg, MB	Zone 3
Saint John, NB	Zone 5	Regina, SK	Zone 2
Quebec City, QC	Zone 4	Edmonton, AB	Zone 3
Montreal, QC	Zone 5	Calgary, AB	Zone 3
Ottawa, ON	Zone 5	Vancouver, BC	Zone 8
Toronto, ON	Zone 6	Victoria, BC	Zone 9

garden credits

Andrew and I would like to extend our sincere thanks to the talented, generous gardeners who accorded us such free and easy access to their outdoor spaces.

Judith Adam: pp. v, 28, 40, 62, 118

Gwynne Basen: p. 12

Dave Benner: pp. 14–15

Andy Black: pp. viii–1

Victor Chanasyk: p. 79

Douglas Counter: pp. 102, 103

Ellen and Robert Eisenberg: pp. v, 36–37, 49, 66, 70, 110–111

Jim French: pp. 43, 44, 74

Wayne and Cathy Gibson: pp. 17, 67

Irene Grosvenor: p. 27

Don and Eileen Herrling: p. 106

Steve Hull: pp. v, vii, 76–77, 80, 92, 101, 104

Lorraine Johnson: pp. v, 98

Michael Kaufman: p. 133

Helen McKean: pp. 20, 131

Stephen Moreland and Linda Kearey: front cover; pp. iv, 114, 123

Bob and Carol Neindorf: p. 34

Amy and David Wilinski: p. 95

Barbara Wilkins: pp. 10, 22, 61, 73

Inga Wood: p. 3

Photographs taken in my own garden appear on pages iii, 6, 47, 50, 53, 55, 58, 65, 69, 83, 85, 88, 91, 97, 109, 117, 121, 130.

index

Acer platanoides 'Crimson King,' 35, 126
Achillea cvs., 13, 81
Achillea millefolium 'Cerise Queen,' 93
acidic soils, 22, 26–27, 30
Ageratina genus, 129
Agriculture Canada, 5, 16
Agropyron repens, 5
Alchemilla mollis, 108, 125
alkaline soils, 23, 30
Alliaria petiolata, 5
alpine columbine, 47
alpine forget-me-nots, 107
altitude, 16
aluminum, 23
Amelanchier spp., 68
American Plants for American Gardens, 11
amorpha (shrub), 29
Amson, Dr. Charles, 108
Amonsia ciliata, 109
Amonsia hubrectii, 109
Amonsia illustris, 109
Amonsia ludoviciana, 109
Amsonia orientalis, 109
Amsonia tabernaemontana, 108–109, 131
Anemone × *hybrida* cvs., 48
Anemone tomentosa 'Superba,' 126, 127
Anemonella thalictroides, 60, 64–67
Antirrhinum majus and cvs., 4
Antirrhinum spp., 48
aphids, 5, 115
Aquilegia alpina, 47
Aquilegia canadensis, 46–47, 81
Aquilegia formosa, 47
Aquilegia longissima, 47
Aquilegia spp., 8, 34, 47, 90, 94
Aquilegia vulgaris, 46, 47
Arctium minus, 5
Argentinean verbena, 34
Arkansas blue star, 109
Arisaema triphyllum, 42
Asarum canadense, 67, *70*
ash, 113
Aster amellus, 99
Aster × *frikartii,* 99

Aster novae-angliae, 79, 94, 97, 99
Aster novi-belgii, 34, 94–99
Aster spp., 94–99
Aster thomsonii, 99
Asteraceae family, 94
astilbe, 125, 135
Astrantia major, 57
Athyrium niponicum var. *pictum,* 116
Atlantic coreopsis, 79
azalea, 23, 30, 48

B
Backwoods of Canada, The (Traill), 41
Banister, John, 100, 102, 132
Baptisia australis, 79, 84–86
Baptisia tinctoria, 84
bare-root (dormant) plants, 38–39
Bartlettina genus, 129
Bath, Trevor, 54, 56
bearded iris, *3*
beebalm, 5, *20,* 79, *94,* 100
bellflowers, 105
'Biedermeier group,' 47
bigroot geranium, 52, 54
birch, 26
black medic, *3,* 5
black-eyed Susan, 79, *94*
black snakeroot, 125
blazingstar, 79, *79, 94*
bleeding heart, 52, 62, *70,* 125, 132
blood meal, 21, 38, 39
bloodroot, 57, 67, 120
blueberry, 23, 26
blue false indigo, 84–86
blue fleabane, 107
blue milkweed, 109
bone meal, 38
boneset, 129, 131
Borage (Boraginaceae) family, 132
bottle gentian, 87–89
Bowden, W.M., 128
'Bowden Hybrids,' 128
Bowles, E.A., 56, 59, 63
broad-leaved plantain, 5

Brown, Lancelot "Capability," 7–8, 23, 24
Bryant, William C., 89
buckeye, 18, 113
buffaloberry, 29
bugleweed, 125
bulbous buttercup, 90
Bulgarian allium, 20–21
buttercups, 46, 90–93
Byzantine gladiolus, 17

C
calcifuges (acid-loving plants), 30
Campanula spp. and cvs., 105
Canada columbine, 46–47, 81
Canadian Crusoes (Traill), 41
Canadian Settler's Guide (Traill), 41
Canadian Wildflowers (Traill), 41
Canadian wild ginger, 67, *70*
carbon:nitrogen ratio, 39
Cardamine pentaphyllos, 52
cardinal flower, 126, 128
Carex spp., 87
carnations and pinks, 4
Carolina silverbell, *27*
carpet bedding designs, 9
Carson, Rachel, 11
cart-track plant, 5
ceonothus (shrub), 26
celandine poppy, 125
Central Park (New York City), 9
Cercis canadensis, 28
Cercis siliquastrum, 28
Charles I, king of England, 46
Chelone spp., 87
Chelsea Physic Garden (London), 8
chickweed, 5
Chinese wisteria, 32
Chionodoxa forbesii, 62
chokeberry, 115
chrysanthemum, 4, 108
Church for the American Colonies, 100
cities, hardiness zones, 144
clay soils, 21, 79
clematis, 31, 84, 124

clear-cutting, 42
clethra, 26
climbing hydrangea, 32, *33*
columbine, 8, 34, 46, 90
common burdock, 5
common mallow, 5
common peony, 4
compass plant, 79, *81*
Compositae family, 94
compost, 23
Compton, Henry, 100
Convallaria majalis, 48, 51
Convulvulus 'Star of Yelta,' 107
Coreopsis tripteris, 79
Cornus spp., 29, 68, 115
Corydalis aurea, 62
Corydalis cava, 60, 63
Corydalis genus, 60
Corydalis lutea, 34, 63
Corydalis sempervirens, 62
Corydalis solida, 60–63, 121, 132
cowslip, 8, *47*, 116–119
crabapple, 68
crabgrass, 5
creeping Jacob's ladder, 59, 81
crown imperial, 48
Culver's root, 129, 131
cup plant, 79
Cypripedium calceolus, 42

D

daffodils, 4, 8, 60, 81, 83, 135
daisy family. *See* Asteraceae family
dame's rocket, 90
damp gardens, 16
    flowering plants, 116–135
    preparing area, 112
    shrubs, 115
    trees, 112, 113
    vines, 31
dandelions, 3, 5
Darmera peltata, 125
Darwin, Charles, 120
daylily, 108, 125
deadheading, 20–21
dead nettle, 48–51
deep-rooted trees/shrubs (native), 18–19
de l'Obel, Mathias, 126
delphiniums, 105
Dendranthema spp. and cvs., 4, 108

Design with Nature (McHaig), 11
Dianthus spp. and cvs., 4
Dianthus barbatus, 8
Dicentra formosa, 52
Dicentra spectabilis, 62, *70*
Dicentra spp., 62, 132
Digitalis purpurea, 52, 116
Digitalis spp. and cvs., 4
Digitaria sanguinalis, 5
Dirr, Michael, 33
Divine Husbandman's Classic, 89
Dodecatheon meadia, 121
dog's-tooth violet, 60
dogwood, 29, 68, 115
dormant plants, 38–39
double Constantinople buttercup, 90
double creeping buttercup, 90–93
doublefile viburnum, *41*
drip hose, 18–19

E

Eastern redbud, *28*
Echinacea angustifolia, 104
Echinacea pallida, 93, 104
Echinacea purpurea, 79, *94, 99,* 100–104, 132
ecology movement, 11
elecampane, 81
elephant's ears, 125
English Flower Garden, The (Robinson), 11
English ivy, 17, 32, 48
English parkland movement, 7–8
Epimedium × *rubrum,* 64, 66
Epimedium × *versicolor* 'Sulfureum,' 66
Erica spp., 30
Erigeron speciosus, 107
Eryngium yuccafolium, 79
Erysimum spp., 8
Eupatorium cannabinum, 130, 131
Eupatorium genus, 129
Euptatorium coelestinum, 131
Eupatorium fistolosum, 129, 131
Eupatorium maculatum, 129, 131
Eupatorium perfoliatum, 129, 131
Eupatorium purpureum, 126, 129–131
Eupatorium rugosum, 131
Euphorbia characias 'Lambrook Gold,' 21
evening primrose, 5, 8
exotic aliens, 2–5
'Explorer' series, 5
European columbine, 46

F

Fabaceae (Legume) family, 84
Fairgrieve, David, 13
false indigo, 79
Farrer, Reginald, 87
ferns, 67
fertilizers, chemical, 11
Filipendula kamtschatica, 107
Filipendula palmata, 107
Filipendula purpurea, 107
Filipendula rubra, 105–107
Filipendula ulmaria, 107
Filipendula vulgaris, 107
fir, 24, 26
Fish, Margery, 30, 46, 56, 59, 63, 93, 109, 124, 126, 130
five-leaved akebia, 32
flowering vines, 32
foam flower, 125
forest(s), 42, 77
Fosteriana tulip, 37
foxglove, 4, 116
Fragaria spp., 52
Fragaria vesca, 8
Franklin, Sir John, 59
French lilac, 45
Frikart, 99
Fritallaria spp., 48

G

Galanthus spp. and cvs., 1, 4, 8
Galium genus, 68
Galium odoratum, 68–71, 129–130
Galium verum, 71
Galtonia candicans, 17
garden design, 7, 30–35
garden phlox, 5, 100
Garden in Wales, A (Johnson), 56
Gardeners Dictionary, The (Miller), 8, 59, 97, 103
Gardeners Kalendar, The (Miller), 8
garlic mustard, 5
Gentiana andrewsii, 87–89
Gentiana genus, 87
Gentiana lutea, 88–89
Gentiana macrophylla, 89
Geranium macrorrhizum, 52, 54
Geranium maculatum, 42, 81
Geranium phaeum, 52, 54
Geranium pratense 'Striatum,' *91,* 93, 123

Geranium spp. and cvs., 21, 52–56, 123, 135
Geranium sylvaticum 'Mayflower,' 55
Gerard, John, 90
Geum aleppicum, 5
Geum triflorum, 81
Gladiolus communis subsp. *byzantinus,* 17
globeflower, 125
glory-of-the-snow, *62*
goatsbeard, 125
golden fumitory, 34, 62
golden groundsel, 123
golden hops, 32
golden spurge, 21, 125
goldenrod, 123
gooseneck loosestrife, 122–124
Granny's bonnet, 47
grape vines, 31
grape-leaved anemone, 127
grasses, 81, 83
great blue lobelia, 126–128
great white trillium, *45*
ground-level plant group, 38
Gunnera manicata, 125

H

Halesia carolina syn. *H. tetraptera, 27*
hardiness zones, 16–17, 143
"hardscape" features, 32, 34
hardy ageratum, 131
hardy chrysanthemum, 108
hawthorn, 18, 28
heartsease, 107
heathers, 23, 30
heaths, 30
Hedera helix, 17, 32, 48
Helianthus spp., 8
Helleborus spp., 57
Hemeracallis spp. and cvs., 108, 125
hemp agrimony, *130,* 131
herbaceous plant group, 32, 38
herbal medicine, 58, 71, 84, 88–89, 100, 104,
    107, 117, 118, 122, 126, 129
Herball (Gerard), 90
Hermann, Paul, 94
Herrick, Robert, 120
Hesperis matronalis, 90
hickory, 18, 24, 113
Himalayan bluebell, 134
Himalayan Jacob's ladder, 58, 59
holly, 25, 27

honesty, 8
honeysuckle, 8, 31
"Hose-in-hose," 120
Hosta spp. and cvs., 4, *17,* 48, *62*
Houttuynia cordata 'Chameleon,' 52
humidity, 17
humus, 23
Hyacinthoides hispanica, 64, 67
hybrid tea roses, 5
hydrangea, 29, 32, 33
Hydrangea petiolaris, 32, 33

I

indigo, 84
Indigofera tinctoria, 84
inorganic mulches, 20
insects, beneficial, 5, 112, 119
Inula helenium, 81
Iris cvs., *3*
iron, 30
ironweed, 79

J

Jack in the green, 120
Jack-in-the-pulpit, *42*
Jacob's ladder, 57–59
James I, king of England, 126
Japanese anemones, 48
Japanese meadow sweet, 107
Japanese painted fern, *116*
Japanese spurge, *37*
Japanese wisteria, 32
jardin anglais, 8
Jefferson, Thomas, 8–9
Jekyll, Gertrude, 132
Jensen, Jens, 11
Joe Pye weed, 126, 129–31
Johnson, A.T., 56
Johnson, Sir William, 126
'Johnson's Blue,' 56
Judas tree, 28
juniper, 19, 25, 29

K

Kalm, Peter, 126
kalmia, 27, *27,* 30
Kirengeshoma palmata, 48, 126, 127
Knautia spp., 8
knot garden, 7
knotweed, 125

L

Lady tulip, 81
lady's mantle, 108, 125
Lamium galeobdolon, 51
Lamium maculatum, 48–51
Lathyrus odoratus and cvs., 4
lavender, 4, 8
leaf blights, 45
leaf mould, 19, 23, 38
Leatherleaf blue star, 109
leaves, fallen, 19, 23, 38, 39
Legume family, 84
Leucanthemum × superbum, 4
Leucojum aestivum, 47, 51
Leucojum spp., 48
Leucojum vernum, 47
Liatris spicata, 79, *79*
Ligularia spp. and cvs., 123
lilac, 4
lilies, 4, 8
Lilium spp. and cvs., 4, 8
lily-of-the-valley, 48, 51
Linnaeus, Carl, 126
Lobelia cardinalis, 126, 128
lobelia cultivars, 128
Lobelia genus, 126
Lobelia siphilitica, 126–128
Lobelia siphilitica f. *albiflora,* 128
Lonicera spp. 8
lords and ladies, 125
Louisiana blue star, 109
Lunaria spp., 8
lungwort, 17, 67, 132
lupines, 84, 108
Lupinus cvs., 84, 108
Lupinus perennis, 81
Lysimachia genus, 122
Lysimachia ciliata 'Purpurea,' 124
Lysimachia clethroides, 122–124
Lysimachia punctata, 122
Lysimachia vulgaris, 122
Lysimachus, king of Thrace, 122
Lythrum salicaria, 3, 5, 122

M

McHarg, Ian, 11
'McKana Hybrids,' 47
Malus spp., 68
Malva neglecta, 5
manganese, 23

manure, composted, 39
maple, 26, 113
marble chips, 20
marjoram, 8
masterwort, 57
May apple, 72
meadow cranesbill, *91*, 93, 123
meadow garden
    flowering plants, 79, 81, 83, 84–109
    grasses, 81, 83
    preparing area, 89
    shrubs, 81, 82
    timing, 78, 81
    vines, 31
meadow rue, 108, 125
Medicago lupulina, 3, 5
Mertens, Franz Karl, 132
Mertensia pulmonarioides, 72, 75, 121,
    132–135
Mertensia sibirica, 134
Mertensia simplicissima, 134
Michaelmas daisy, 34, 94–99
micro-climates, 17
micronutrients, 21, 30
micro-organisms, 23, 30, 39
mildew, 45
milky bellflower, 125
Miller, Philip, 8, 30, 59, 97, 103
Ministry of Agriculture and Food, 30
Miscanthus sinensis 'Zebrinus,' 83
Mithridates Eupator, king of Pontus, 129
Monarda didyma, 5, *20, 94*
Monticello, gardens at, 9
Mount Royal (Montreal), 9
mountain bluebell, l32, 134
mountain laurels, 30
mountain mint, 100
mourning widow, 54
'Mrs. Scott-Elliot Hybrids,' 47
mulches, 19–21
My Garden in Summer (Bowles), 56
Myosotis alpestris, 107
Myosotis sylvestris, 60

N

Narcissus poeticus var. *recurvus, 83*
Narcissus spp. and cvs., 4, 8, 60, 81, 135
native grasses, 83
native plants, 2
native trees/shrubs, 24–29

native vines, 31
naturalized gardens
    designing, 30–35
    history of, 7–13
    principles of, vii, 2–6, 30
    recommended plants, historic, 8
    styles, 35 (*See also* damp gardens;
        natural meadows; woodland gadens)
natural meadows, 16
natural succession, 45
Necterosordum siculum, 21
New England aster, 79, 94, 97, 99
New York aster, 34, 94–99
Nichols, Beverley, 30
nitrogen, 21, 39
nodding trillium, 73, 75
non-native vines, 32
Norway maple, 35, 126
nutrients, 21

O

oak, 18, 24, 25, 26, 28, 113
obedient plant, 125
*Oecology of Plants: An Introduction to the Study
    of Plant Communities* (Warming), 11
Oenothera spp. and cvs., 5, 8
Olmstead, Frederick Law, 9
Oriental hybrid lilies, 4
Oriental poppies, *3, 4*
Origanum majorana, 8
Ornithogalum nutans, 1
Our Lady's bedstraw, 71
Oxford Botanic Garden, 52, 100, 132
oyster plant, 132, 134

P

'Pacific Giant' series, 120
Paeonia lactiflora, 4
Paeonia spp., 8, 84
Paeonia × smouthii, 107
painted trillium, 75
pale corydalis, 62
pale purple coneflower, 93, 104
Papaver orientale, 3, 4
Paradisea liliastrum, 46–47, 51
parkland movement, 7–9
'Parkland' series, 5
Pasque flower, 81
peat moss, 20
Pelargonium spp., 52

Penstemon digitalis, 79
peonies, 8, 84
perennial sweet pea, 32
Perilla frutescens var. *crispa,* 116
periwinkle, *37*
Persian buttercup, 90
pesticides, 11, 13
pH, 22, 30, 30, 39
Phlox divaricata, 42
Phlox paniculata, 5, 100
phosphorus, 21
photoperiodism, 94
Physostegia virginiana, 102
pine, 19, 24, 26
Plantago major, 5
Plantago spp., 3
plantain lily, 3, 4, 125
plant groups, 31–32
Pliny, 122
Podophyllum peltatum, 72
poet's narcissus, *83*
Polemonium caeruleum, 57–59
Polemonium caeruleum var. *lacteum,* 58
Polemonium caeruleum 'Brise d'Anjou,' 57,
    58–59
Polemonium genus, 57
Polemonium humile, 59
Polemonium 'Lambrook Mauve,' 59
Polemonium reptans, 59, 81
Polemonium × richardsonii, 59
polysaccharides, 129
ponds, 112, *115*
Populus albus, 126
porcelain berry, 32
Portulaca oleracea, 5
potassium, 21
prairie ecosystems, 78
prairie plants, 79, 81
Prairie smoke, 81
precipitation, 17–19
primrose, 4, 8, 60, 119–120
Primula genus, 116–120
Primula spp. and cvs., 4, 60, 119
Primula veris, 8, *47,* 116–119
Primula vulgaris, 4, 8, 119–120
Primulaceae family, 122, 123
privacy, 34–35, 81, 82
Pulmonaria cvs., 17
Pulmonaria genus, 67, 132
Pulsatilla patens, 81

purple avens, 125
purple coneflower, 79, *94*, *99*, 100–104, 132
purple corydalis, 121, 132
purple foxglove, 52
purple fumewort, 60–63
purple loosestrife, 3, 5, 122
purple morning glory 107
purple perilla, 116
purslane, 5
Puschkinia scilloides, 1, 62
Pychanthemum virginianum, 100

Q
Qin jiao, 89
quackgrass, 5
Queen of the prairie, 87, 105–107

R
Ranunculaceae family, 46
Ranunculus genus, 90
Ranunculus acris 'Flore Pleno,' 90
Ranunculus asiaticus, 90
Ranunculus bulbosus, 90
Ranunculus constantinoplitanus 'Plenus,' 90
Ranunculus repens 'Pleniflorus,' 90–93
Ranunculus spp., 81
Ratibida pinnata, 79
rattlesnake master, 79
Reading Agricultural College (U.K.), 70
red barrenwort, 66
red trillium, 73, 75
Rheum palmatum, 125
rhododendron, 23, 27, 30, 48
Rhododendron spp. and cvs., 30, 48
Richardson, John, 59
Robinson, William, 9, 11, 21, 56, 63, 72, 97,
    99, 124, 132
Rodgersia aesculifolia, 125
Rosa gallica versicolor, 7
Rosa spp., 8
Rosaceae (Rose) family, 5, 8, 105
Royal Botanic Society (U.K.), 9
Royal Horticultural Society Gardens (U.K.),
    128
Rudbeckia genus, 102, 103
Rudbeckia hirta, 79, *94*
Rudbeckia laciniata, 46
rue anemone, 60, 64–67

S
Sackville-West, Vita, 7
St. Bruno's lily, 46–47, 51
salmon Jacob's ladder, 58, 59
salt marsh hay, 20
sandy soils, 21, 23, 39
Sanguinaria canadensis, 57, 67, 120
Scabiosa spp., 8
scabious, 8
Scilla siberica, 1
self-seeding, 20–21
serviceberries, 68
Shakespeare, William, 90, 119
shasta daisy, 4
shooting star, 81, 121
showy sunflower, 79
shrubs (native)
    acidic soils, 26–27
    alkaline soils, 29
    damp garden, 115
    deep-rooted, 19, 23
    longest-lived, 25
    meadow garden, 81, 82
    woodland garden, 42, 45
Siberian bugloss, 125
Siberian iris, 125
Siberian squill, 1
Silent Spring (Carson), 11
Silphium laciniatum, 79, *81*
Silphium perfoliatum, 79
silt, 23
smooth penstemon, 79
snake's-head fritillary, 125
snapdragons, 4, 48
snowberry, 29
snowdrops, 1, 4, 8
snowflake, 48, 125
soaker hose, 18–19
soil, 21, 23
Solidago cvs., 123
Spanish bluebells, *64,* 67
spiderwort, 46, 81, 93, 125
Spiraea genus, 8, 105
spotted geranium, *42,* 81
spring ephemerals, 60, 132
spring snowflake, 47
sprinklers, 18–19
spruce, 24, 26
squirrel corn, 62
Stachys officinalis, 57

stamens, 120
Star-of-Bethlehem, *1*
State Department of Agriculture, 30
Stellaria media, 5
stigmas, 120
stinging nettle, 48
strawberries, 52
streams, 112
striped squill, 1, 62
Studies of Plant Life in Canada (Traill), 41, 42
Stylophorum diphyllum, 72
summer hyacinth, 17
summer snowflake, 47, *51*
sunflowers, 8
sweet alyssum, 94
sweet peas, 4, 84
sweet violets, *47,* 48
sweet william, 8
sweet woodruff, 68–71, 129–30
Syringa spp. and cvs., 4
Syringa vulgaris, 45

T
tall lungwort, 134
tap-rooted trees, 18–19
Taraxacum officinale, 3, 5
temperature, 16–17
Temple Coffee House Botanists' Club, 100
Thalictrum spp., 108, 125
Thomas, Graham Stuart, 62, 68, 87, 93, 99,
    107, 109, 128
toad lily, 87, 125
toad trillium, 75
topsoil, 21, 23, 39
Tradescant, John, Jr., 46
Tradescant, John, Sr., 46
Tradescantia ohiensis, 81, *93*
Tradescantia virginiana, 46
Traill, Catherine Parr, 41–42, 63, 75,
    89, 104, 126, 129
trees, *17,* 18–19, 23, 24–29, 35,
    42, 45, 112, 113
Tricyrtis spp. and cvs., 87, 125
trillium, 72–75
Trillium cernuum, 73
Trillium cuneatum, 73
Trillium erectum, 73
Trillium grandiflorum, 45, 72, *73,* 75
Trillium spp., 72–75
Tulip clusiana, 81

Tulipa 'Madame Lefeber' syn. 'Red Emperor,' *37*
Tulipa spp. and cvs., 4, 48, 90
turtleheads, 87

U
Urtica dioica, 48
U.S. Department of Agriculture (USDA), 16
U.S. hardiness zones, 16
Uvularia grandiflora, 75

V
valerian, 58
Valeriana officinalis, 58
variegated kiwi, 32
variegated sedges, 87
vegetables, *13*
Verbena bonariensis, 34, 94
Veronica noveboracensis, 79
Veronicastrum virginicum, 129, 131
viburnum, 28
Viburnum plicatum subsp. *tomentosum* 'Mariesii,' *41*
Vinca minor, 37
vines, 31–32, *33*
Viola spp., 8
Viola odorata, 47, 48
Viola tricolor, 107
violets, 8
Virginia bluebells, 72, *75*, 121, 132–135

von Bergzabern, Jakob Theodore, 108

W
wallflower, 8
walnut, 19, 28
Warming, Eugenius, 11
watering methods, 18–19
weeds, 13
western white trillium, 75
white-man's foot, 5
white mugwort, 125
white poplar tree, 126
white snakeroot, 131
white trillium, 73, 75, *75*
whorled loosestrife, 122
Wild Garden, The (Robinson), 9, 11, 56
wild indigo, 84
wildlife, 31, 38, 34, 77, 78, 81, 103, 104, 115
wild lupine, 81
willow, 113
willow blue star, 108–109, 131
winter hardy roses, 5
wisteria, 32
wood betony, 57
woodland daffodil, *75*
woodland forget-me-not, 60
Woodland Garden, A (Johnson), 56
woodland gardens, 16
    flowering plants, 46–75
    maintaining, 45

preparing area, 38
timing, 38–41, 42
trees/shrubs, 42, 45
vines, 31
woodland geranium, 55
woodland phlox, *42*
woodland strawberry, 8
wood poppies, 72
woody plant group, 31–32, 38–41
Wright, Frank Lloyd, 11

Y
yarrow, *13*, 81, 91, 93
yellow archangel, 51
yellow avens, 5
yellow barrenwort, *66*
yellow coneflower, 46, 79, 100
yellow corydalis, 62
yellow loosestrife, 122
yellow wax-bells, 48, 126, 127

Z
zebra grass, 83, 129
zinc, 30
zones, hardiness, 16–17, 144